O9-BUB-242

*"That town you passed through,
it's not called Schittsville, it's called Schitt's Creek.
And, it's where we live."*

JOHNNY ROSE

FAN ART BY CARA MATHIS

FAN ART BY JESSICA CRUICKSHANK

BEST WISHES, WARMEST REGARDS

THE STORY OF SCHITT'S CREEK

DANIEL LEVY and **EUGENE LEVY**

BLACK DOG
& LEVENTHAL
PUBLISHERS
NEW YORK

BEHIND THE SCENES
Eugene Levy and Daniel Levy on set for episode 607, "Moira Rosé."
June 3, 2019

INTRODUCTION

WHEN WE WERE FIRST APPROACHED about putting a book together we asked ourselves the same question that was raised when we first started making *Schitt's Creek* over seven years ago: what can we do with this opportunity? Our original answer was a simple one: tell stories that make us laugh about people we want to root for. Little did we know that would result in eighty episodes of laughter and tears, growth and love, risk and reward. And that was just behind the scenes!

Somehow, along the way, we also met you, our loyal viewers. Although "loyal" feels like an understatement. To be blunt, we simply wouldn't be here if it weren't for your generosity, passion, and steadfast support of the stories we were telling. Over the years we've tried to read every letter you've sent us, every tweet on Tweeters, every strange and wonderful piece of fan art you made honoring our cast, because you have become a part of our television family. So when we thought about this book and asked ourselves, "What can we do with this opportunity?" the answer was simple: thank all of you for helping make this show what it is today.

And with that we have spent nearly two years attempting to perfect this little token of our appreciation by pulling back the curtain on all the fun we had making the show.

So, cheers to you.

With our best wishes and our warmest regards,

DAN AND EUGENE LEVY

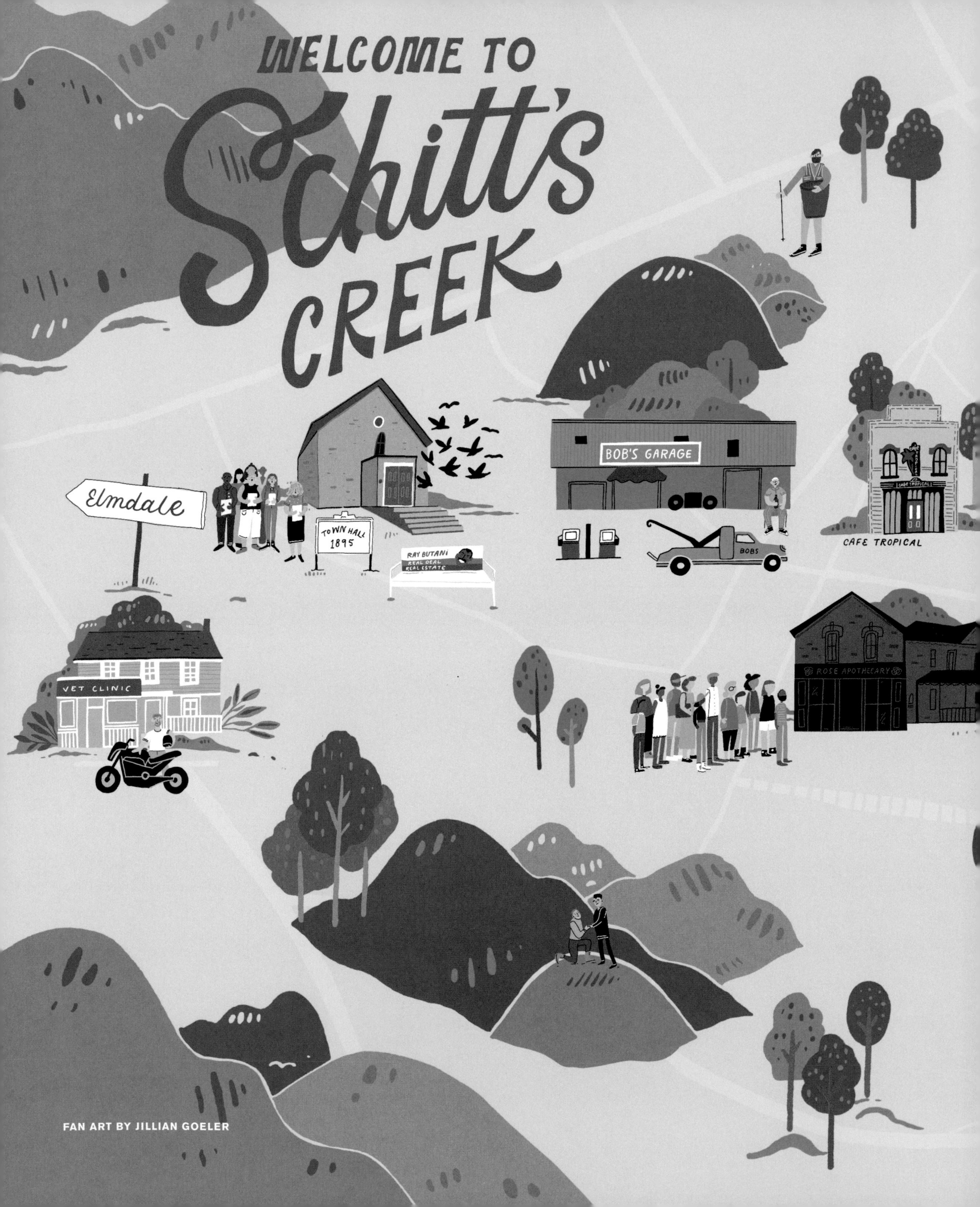

WELCOME TO Schitt's CREEK

Elmdale

TOWN HALL 1895

RAY BUTANI
REAL DEAL
REAL ESTATE

BOB'S GARAGE

BOBS

CAFE TROPICAL

VET CLINIC

ROSE APOTHECARY

FAN ART BY JILLIAN GOELER

FAN ART BY ROSS COOKE

CREATING A CAST OF CHARACTERS

EUGENE LEVY: Launching *Schitt's Creek* was the most fascinating part of this whole journey for me. It began with an invitation from my son, Daniel, to work with him on developing a TV show, something I thought would never be in the cards. I took it upon myself to make absolutely sure I would come through for him. And so, I listened to his idea about a wealthy family who lose everything.

His rationale, that Reality TV has already formed our perspective of the way wealthy families function, was definitely on point. It puts us in position as the fly on the wall, observing how these family members relate to each other when funds are unlimited and opulence is the comforting blanket that keeps them all safe and secure.

But what would it be like to be a fly on the wall, observing these people if all the money was suddenly gone? This was at the nub of Daniel's very solid idea. And so, we embarked on what turned out to be more than just a father-son project. It had all the makings of a very interesting, very funny, character-based show.

I knew from watching Daniel's work for seven years on MTV Canada that he was exceptionally relaxed on live television. He was smart, funny, and knew how to promote the strongest aspects of who he was as a person. His sketch work, both as a writer and performer, continued to mature comedically over the years. In my eyes he was the strongest, most charismatic host they had. What I didn't know was whether he had what it takes to write and perform a weekly half-hour comedy, where character has to be strong enough and consistent enough to attract and hold its viewers every single week.

Working on our presentation pilot showed me just how strongly he was coming into his own as a writer, particularly a writer who had his finger on the pulse of his own generation. His work on camera showed me in the most vivid way just how entrenched he was, as an actor, in his own character of David Rose. I was totally confident, if we could sell our pilot, that Daniel would be as strong a creative partner as anyone with years more experience than he.

Launching our first season on CBC was exciting in so many ways. Our scripts were solid, our cast was exceptionally talented, and our sets and locations gave the show its personality. The thing that stood out the most to me in that first season, as was the case in every season, was working on the family scenes.

Shooting the Rose family scenes, in those two motel rooms, with Catherine, Annie, and Daniel, proved to be the most fun, rewarding, and heartfelt for me. Those scenes were the bedrock of *Schitt's Creek*.

The other thing that struck me about our first season was the combination of script and performance and just how beautifully they melded to give the show the most idyllic sensibility. We laughed at and with the Roses, but we were also starting to feel something for the Roses. It became so quickly evident that the character-driven comedy that Daniel and I set out to make was already superseding our grandest expectations. It was the perfect launching pad to give the show its ultrabright future.

DANIEL LEVY: I have long admired my Dad's work with Christopher Guest in redefining and refining the mockumentary genre. The time and care they put into writing those movies built the perfect foundation upon which a brilliant troop of actors could shine. The movies were indisputably funny, but they were also kind and warm and hopeful, with characters that were realized, flawed, and lovable.

Because I knew *Schitt's Creek* needed that kind of character-driven energy to elevate it from a slapstick sitcom to a more nuanced, single camera comedy, I asked him if he'd be into discussing the idea of working together. Fortunately, he agreed to sit down with me and over the course of several weekends we began to build a show. That process started out slow—very slow. The exercise of figuring out who these characters would be was a long one, but it was also, as I came to realize, a necessary one. We would spend weeks brainstorming a single character: "Where did they go to school? Who were their parents? Were they happy babies?" By the end of the process we knew every single thing about each character in the show. In fact, Alexis's short-lived reality show, *A Little Bit Alexis*, was born from one of those early brainstorming sessions.

As anxious as I was to just start writing the scripts, my Dad insisted that nailing down the characters was going to make the writing easier. He was right. How fortunate we were to then find a cast that would elevate all that work we did to hilarious, meaningful, and emotional new heights. This show is a celebration of those characters. What a time we all had bringing them to life.

JOHNNY ROSE

"My family and I have been staying in a motel for the past three years. And I wouldn't trade our stay there for anything."

by
EUGENE LEVY

PLAYING JOHNNY ROSE was one of the most interesting experiences I've had as an actor because of the subtleties involved in Johnny's evolution from a man immersed in an opulent lifestyle to a man immersed in his family. It was an evolution from thinking that being a good father was sending his kids to the best boarding schools and hiring the best nannies, to the realization that over the last few years in Schitt's Creek, through all the hardship and under his mentoring, his kids turned out to be independent, responsible, fully functioning, loving human beings.

But the most challenging aspect of playing Johnny for me was the fact that it was the polar opposite of what I had built a career doing— namely character work based solely on getting laughs. There was always a comfort in playing characters that sported a different physical appearance from my own. Mustaches, soul patches, fake teeth, and a variety of eyewear were involved. So, being the straight man on *Schitt's Creek*, and looking very much like myself, was an exciting yet frightening change of pace. My job now was not so much being responsible for getting laughs as it was being responsible for others getting theirs. I was playing the anchor that grounds not only the Rose family but also the show, and I embraced that responsibility wholeheartedly.

If there is one thing I would most want fans to remember about Johnny, his epitaph so to speak, it would be how heroically he carried himself through a devastatingly tragic time for him and his family. He was a man who mustered all his skill as a CEO of the second largest video rental chain in North America, and combined it with his greatest virtue— patience. He was also able to guide his family through what they thought to be their darkest days, but ultimately turned out to be their brightest.

MOIRA ROSE

"Never let the bastards get you down!"

by
CATHERINE O'HARA

NO MATTER HOW PEOPLE may think Moira changed or evolved over the years, she and I always knew how wonderful she could be. She believes she is seriously creative in the arts and that she has just not yet been given enough opportunities to fulfill her bountiful potential. Her daily wardrobe and hair choices not only remind herself and others of who she really is, but they are her art form, expressing both her creativity and her inner emotional life. With her sartorial efforts and her vocabulary, she is sharing her love of all things beautiful with anyone lucky enough to be in her presence.

So many stories written for characters past a certain age involve death, divorce, and disease. Sadly, those experiences are the reality if you're lucky enough to live a long life, but thanks to our great scripts, Moira is allowed so many fresh, new, crazy, dramatic, silly, and fun adventures, the greatest being the opportunity to shed her old life and start anew with her family.

She believes she's a great mother but has no idea how fortunate she is to have been given this second chance to get to know and fall in love with her children. She loves and respects Johnny. She believes she provides the excitement in their marriage, but is grateful for his unconditional love, his wisdom, and his even temperament. Loving wife that she is, she never blames him for hiring the business manager who ripped their lives out from under them. I, for one, would like to be more like Moira.

Daniel, Eugene, and I agreed, though, that Moira would never totally embrace life in the town and would be the one to keep her family on course to one day get out of there. (She never once said the name of the town aloud.)

DAVID ROSE

"Like Beyoncé, I excel as a solo artist. And I was also dressed by my mother well into my teens."

by
DANIEL LEVY

DAVID'S JOURNEY over the course of the six seasons of the show was one of self-discovery and realizing that he doesn't have to be defined by the social circles he surrounds himself with and the places he travels. At his core, I think he really doubted who he was and turned to fashion and fake friends as a means of creating a lifestyle for himself, because I think he thought that was interesting, or more interesting than what he had to offer. In actuality, what we learn over these six seasons is that he has a lot to offer. He just needed a safe space to reveal himself.

Getting to play him was such a gift. It was a very slow but steady journey toward letting people in, one at a time, and then ultimately finding the love of his life in the most unlikely of places. He is a character that has taught me a lot. To get to say the kinds of things that he says, to get to be as reactive as he is, was really enlightening for me on a personal level. In a lot of ways, I have walked away from this show a more self-assured and confident person because of David Rose. Whether he knows it or not, he's a very authentic person, despite being a ball of anxiety and insecurity. He had the confidence in him the whole time, he just didn't know it.

I miss him a lot. I miss getting to put on his clothes. I miss his attitude. I miss being able to let off my own personal steam through him. The process of becoming David Rose every day was an instant transformation. It was so comforting to put those clothes on each morning—those Rick Owens lace-up boots and whatever skirt was at my disposal—and walk out onto set very much ready for the day.

I remember taking those shoes off for the last time on our last day and really having a moment where I thanked David for all the work he had done for me. You become so close to the characters that you play, especially when you play them for 80 episodes of television. To say goodbye really did feel like I was saying goodbye to someone I knew and loved. It was a very tough thing that last day, taking the costume off and putting it on a couch and saying, "Well, until we meet again."

ALEXIS ROSE

*"I don't skate through life, David. I walk through life,
in really nice shoes."*

by
ANNIE MURPHY

THINKING ABOUT ALEXIS has me smiling like a proud mother. First of all, being on *Schitt's Creek* was truly the best time of my life. Being able to play a strong, funny female character who developed and changed so drastically over the course of six seasons was an experience that I'd never had before. It was an experience that was so incredibly wonderful and helped me grow so much as a person.

When we meet Alexis, she is a real handful and not necessarily the most likable person. She's self-absorbed and obsessed with boys and, let's say, the finer things in life. I don't think she was someone who had many relationships that went deeper than just scratching the surface. Then when we leave her, she has discovered what friendship means and what love means. She's become a far more selfless person. She's pursued an education. She's pursued a career. She is a core member of the family that she's come to love so much. It was such a pleasure to play that arc. It was also really fun being a bit of a selfish brat. Who throws a muffin at someone to get their attention? Alexis Rose does in season one! Seeing her confidence grow while at the same time watching her care and concern and consideration of other people grow made her a very, very special character.

I find myself crying about missing the show and the people on it probably once or twice a month. I'm so lucky because I know that the friendships I made on the show will last a lifetime, but you still have to say goodbye to these characters. Watching Catherine in her last scene as Moira, knowing that I might never see Moira again, or Twyla or Ted, was so tough. Even though they're fictional characters, they've become so important and special to me. To have to hang up those costumes and put those people on a shelf felt like I was losing a little part of myself.

STEVIE BUDD

"I'm only doing this because you called me rude.
And I take that as a compliment."

by
EMILY HAMPSHIRE

I ONLY FOUND OUT much later that Stevie was named after Stevie Nicks. That was the backstory that I never got to read. When I first got the part, I had no idea that she was going to be all that she is, which I think is also the same journey that Stevie went on. I thought I was going to be the girl behind the desk who says sarcastic things and brings the family towels. That's what I thought I was signing up for. Then over the course of the seasons, this girl, who at the beginning was this really hard shell, began to have her layers peeled back and we realize that, oh my god, there's like a real girl inside! That to me is Stevie. She was always this super authentic, vulnerable person who built up all these protective mechanisms around her, but at her core she could see people like David for who they really were inside.

I think Stevie is also the audience. Most people know more "Stevies" than anyone from the Rose family. So, especially for the first season, a lot of Stevie's role is being the audience watching this crazy family, these kind of alien creatures who come into town, and then getting to know who they really are.

She also doesn't put on any airs. She doesn't find value in pretending to be something bigger than she thinks she should be, which is what I love the most about Stevie. She's just got this quiet confidence and, like Moira says to her at the end, "You're so cool. You just stand your solid ground, refusing to be anything but you." It was really interesting with Stevie. I found that from the beginning I got such a stillness from her that I don't always have in life, but I loved it when I had it with Stevie.

ROLAND SCHITT

"I'm the mayor, so if you're looking for an ass to kiss, it's mine."

by
CHRIS ELLIOTT

WHEN EUGENE first called me to see if I'd be interested in doing *Schitt's Creek,* I said, "Yes!" automatically before even knowing anything about the show. Who in their right mind would turn down the opportunity to work with Eugene Levy and Catherine O'Hara? And then when I heard who the character was, I was ecstatic. Roland was right up my alley.

Besides some wardrobe touches, a padded belly, and the *business in the front, party in the back* wig, everything about Roland was already on the page when I read the first script. Still, it was a bit of a challenge for me to make him semi-believable and, dare I say, semi-*likable?* I mean, here's a guy who has an exaggerated sense of his self-worth, who's blissfully unaware of what other people are thinking about him, and who never takes the temperature of a room before blurting out whatever's on his mind. Roland can be exacerbating, egotistical, rude, and, of course, thick as a rock, but beneath it all, I think Roland is insecure. It's only as the series progresses that we catch little glimpses into his vulnerable nature. Those glimpses help make the character more three-dimensional.

The one person who understands Roland's sensitive side (for lack of a better word) is his wife, Jocelyn. She's his rock. Roland relies on Jocelyn for everything. The two have probably been together since high school and are as much in love today as they were back then. It's her devotion to him that buys Roland the benefit of the doubt from the audience. Because we see him being a good husband, a good dad, and caring for people in his own way, Roland grows on us and, eventually (maybe by season six), becomes, dare I say, semi-*likable?*

JOCELYN SCHITT

"We all have fears as parents, Moira, but at some point, we just have to believe in our kids."

by
JENNIFER ROBERTSON

I LOVE JOCELYN, and I miss her. Jocelyn and I have things in common, as most actors will say about a character, and there are things that we do not have in common. Jocelyn is much more patient and much more pragmatic than I am. But, similar to her, I do like to find the positives about people, and that's one of the great things about Jocelyn. She looks for the best in people and sees beyond. I think that's why she's a schoolteacher. Great teachers bring out the best in kids and recognize them for the individuals that they are. They go with the flow, and that's certainly her personality.

Jocelyn was able to be friends with Moira from the day she arrived, and that's not an easy friendship! Moira was a wild new person in her life, but if you think about it, her husband is also a little wild. So, I think Jocelyn does well with big personalities. I would say she is able to take them in, but not let them overtake her. She can really stand her ground with big personalities, even when they're being very self-centered.

When I did character prep for the audition, I watched videos of Jackie Kennedy touring the White House. To see her pride in being the partner of someone who is an important political leader, whether it's president of the United States or, in Jocelyn's case, the mayor of Schitt's Creek, was very instructive. And the Schitts can claim family legacy! They're essentially the Kennedys of Schitt's Creek. Jocelyn liked that idea very much and she settled into that role quite naturally.

RONNIE LEE

"I've got perfect pitch, so do not
mess this up for me."

by
KAREN ROBINSON

I THINK RONNIE REALLY, really loves her town. I think she chooses to live there. With her savvy and skill set, and, you know, a change of wardrobe, she could really be anywhere, but she chooses to wear what she wears and live in Schitt's Creek. She loves her chosen family there, and that includes the Roses, who evolve into being a part of her chosen family, and she really loves her life and lives it the way she chooses.

Preparing to play Ronnie was relatively easy because it's the most comfortable that I've been on set in costume. Ronnie was all about being real and being herself. There was no waistline that needed to be stitched, no cheekbones that needed to be highlighted, or hair that needed to be shellacked. She was clean and presentable and wore natural fibers, which I love. The other part of it was that I basically channeled my mother's face for the role. My mother makes much different sartorial choices than Ronnie. She's much more glamorous, but her face betrays her thoughts, and whatever she says confirms what she's thinking. I used that a lot with Ronnie, because she could not help but let you know, when the time was right, exactly what was going on in her head. That was extremely helpful.

I think people should strive to be more like Ronnie. Live your life authentically. When you speak, speak the truth. I think everybody needs a friend like her. She will tell you what's up in no uncertain terms. The Ronnies of this world are a valuable part of society. They are the ones who, damn the consequences, they're gonna tell you how they feel, because they have a singular, strong sense of self. So listen to Ronnie: when you hear that little voice talking to you, saying, "This party is over, and it's time to move on." I feel like that was Ronnie's gift. She always knew when to exit a scene.

TWYLA SANDS

"It's about how you live your life.
Doing what makes you smile."

by
SARAH LEVY

TWYLA, OH GOSH, BLESS HER. Twyla has always been a big question mark, because sometimes she's sharp as a tack and right on the mark and other times she is completely clueless. I'd never know which way she was going to swing. The writers definitely kept me on my toes. The biggest constant, though, is her genuine take on the world, which is that of love and kindness. We've learned so much about her dark past and her family history, all things that could easily drive someone to see the world through a very depressing lens. Yet, she chose to move forward with positivity, empathy, and light, something that exemplifies how strong a woman she is. It's always been my favorite thing about her.

I wasn't aware of any huge parallels between our personalities, but many people have pointed out that we're both eternally sunny. As much as I would love to agree with that, I think I've learned so much more from Twyla than she would have learned from me. Twyla has this incredible patience that I've tried to adopt in my own life that I think is extremely useful, especially when having conversations with people about topics and issues on which we don't necessarily agree. Twyla has never been one to shame another person, and I think that's why Alexis, consciously or unconsciously, has chosen to confide in her so frequently.

My dad has always said that Twyla is the heartbeat of the town, and as the seasons went on, the more I tended to agree with this. She embodies everything the town represents: openness, inclusiveness, and supportiveness. The café was also the vehicle for those attitudes in so many ways. There were so many memories created at that counter and in those booths, and to be so closely associated with that environment is an honor.

RAY BUTANI

"Remind me, are you here for a photo series or travel planning or our newest service, closet organization?"

by
RIZWAN MANJI

THE ROLE OF RAY is one of the few jobs that I got without an audition. I had been on the show *Outsourced* and I had done some other stuff, so I had a demo reel. I think Eugene Levy was like, "Yeah, this is the guy."

Ray is an optimist and an opportunist. He was a travel agent, a closet organizer, a Christmas tree salesman, a photographer, a videographer, an auctioneer. He rented out his spare room, so he was kind of like a landlord. He also briefly served on Town Council and he has a podcast.

I loved playing Ray because he's one of those characters who makes you feel happy because he's so happy. So, when you play him, you have to find that feeling even when you're not in that kind of a mood.

Ray also loves to be in the mix. I know he comes across as annoying to people, but he just loves interaction and there's something about it that's infectious. Sometimes there are weird things happening in your own life and you're not exactly in a good place, but just playing Ray helped me get to that place, because he just loves being alive.

PATRICK BREWER

"I've spent most of my life not knowing what 'right' was supposed to feel like. And then I met you and everything changed."

by
NOAH REID

I THINK THE FIRST THING I NOTICED about Patrick when I went in for the audition was that he was a very together, very confident guy, but in a low-key kind of way and with an innate kindness and acceptance. He has a sharp sense of humor, a bit of an edge, and he enjoys the immediate chemistry and gamesmanship of the evolving relationship with David. That was the thing that I immediately hooked into—a bit of a sarcastic, wry sense of humor, a comfort in his own skin, and a confidence that things will probably work out and that he will have some sense of control over how things go.

Patrick is the kind of person who takes things as they are and appreciates how strange and wonderful and ridiculous any given situation might be. He has the ability to bird's-eye-view the state of things, make a quick joke, and then see what to do about it. I've just had so much fun with that. Right off the top, it felt like there were a lot of very playable moments, especially with Dan. Dan is such an expressive comedic actor, he's a very reactive guy, and David's a very reactive personality. It was fun to watch him dig himself into a hole and then to push him a little farther into the hole and watch him react to that, before throwing him a rope and helping him out of it. I feel like we were always playing a little game with each other whenever we were in scenes together.

There's an interesting thing that happens when you've played a character over a long stretch of time: you form a bond with them, like you have a shared purpose, and when the show comes to an end, your shared goal has been completed. So you let them go, but you don't have to say goodbye to them because they exist outside of you, they live in that world that you've created together. Of course any actor is going to bring elements of their own personality and life to a character that they play, and I think Dan liked pulling out little pieces of the cast's lives to enhance their characters. I think Patrick's aggressively competitive streak was an element of my own personality that became an element of Patrick's personality. And those blurred lines become a shared territory. Patrick's not me, and I'm not him, but, to paraphrase the great Mariah Carey, he'll always be a part of me, and I'm part of him indefinitely. We're interlocked but not interchangeable.

TED
MULLENS

"I do have tur-tell *you that I've been thinking about you, a lot."*

by
DUSTIN MILLIGAN

TED HAS BEEN such an interesting character to play. One of the things I've always loved about him is how much he's grown throughout the entire six seasons of the show.

It's mostly through Ted's relationship with Alexis that we've gotten to understand him. I don't think Ted was really ready for Alexis in the beginning. I'm a gymnast, so a metaphor I often apply to Ted is that it's like he tried to start off on the rings without being ready for them. He proposed to Alexis for the first time way too soon, in season one and, just like the rings in gymnastics, if you're not actually ready for them, if you're not strong enough, you will be in for a world of hurt. That's what happened with Ted. He tried to go that route, naïvely, and ambitiously, and neither of them was ready for that.

As a result, all through seasons two and three he was kind of just bouncing around trying to recover himself. He went from butch biker guy to dating an artisanal cheese-making farm woman. There were a lot of ups and downs until he was finally able to commit and try again for Alexis in a complete way at the end of season four.

There was a lot of discovery there. They finally became grounded together, and it was like they knew where they stood with each other. They were both able to admit to some mistakes they'd made, and once they could do that, they became a really beautiful pair, in perfect sync with each other. Suddenly they're feeding each other and complementing each other, and there's a lot of comedy that came out of it, but also a lot of heart, which I think is what made their breakup powerful, but also something that the audience was able to accept and support.

Knowing that they always had each other's best interests at heart was such a beautiful thing. So, as painful as the dismount from that relationship was, it was necessary and so wonderful to see them have that moment together.

BOB CURRIE

*"Oh jeez, to be a fly on the wall
for this conversation."*

by
JOHN HEMPHILL

TO BE HONEST, I'm not one to think about my character all that much, it just kind of happens. So, with Bob, I just started playing him. Fortunately, early on in the first season there was a moment when I had to run out from Bob's Garage to see Johnny. I remember it was quite a long run and I thought to myself, well jeez, I've got to do something to make this interesting. So, spur of the moment, I just kind of came up with a goofy run, which wasn't exactly a run, but more like a shimmy. It ended up really appealing to me, and as soon as I did it, I suddenly felt very at home with the character. It just gave me this attitude that made me think, I might have something here.

Bob has that quality of the kind of *Honeymooners* archetype. He's a good-hearted guy but also always on the lookout for a little money on the side. He loved his wife. His business was good, but he wouldn't turn down an opportunity to make a buck.

With respect to Johnny and the Roses, I think Bob embraced them. He immediately offered Johnny a place to set up in his garage, not without a catch of course, but it showed that Bob was an accepting guy. I think he and Johnny really became friends.

It was also fantastic to work with Eugene Levy. We've worked together on a number of things over the years and he's just such a funny guy. He has such a good sense of what's funny and what's not. And Catherine too. I hadn't worked with her since *Really Weird Tales*, so it was great to work with both of them again. And Chris Elliott made me laugh for so many years, and I was a huge fan of his father, so it was a real treat to work with him as well.

Working on the show was a joy. I don't act all that much, so when I get the opportunity, I totally embrace it. I met a lot a nice people on *Schitt's Creek,* so it really was just a lot of fun.

MUTT
SCHITT

"We sat down and we spoke our truths. Pretty freeing.
That day I picked 700 cones."

by
TIM ROZON

MUTT IS A MYSTERIOUS character right off the bat. He definitely had an interesting past. He lives in a barn, he composts, but he doesn't know what he's supposed to do with himself, so in that sense he's a little lost. We get the sense that his dad, Roland, was kind of disappointed in him, because Mutt didn't want to be the mayor of Schitt's Creek. Nobody likes to feel that they disappointed their parents, that's for sure. So, I think there's a bit of that going on, and that's maybe why he was lost, but those are the great mysteries that we'll never know about Mutt.

The thing that I love about Mutt is that he's just so dependable. The best way I can describe him is like a comfortable old pair of boots. That's how it felt to play him. I never felt more at ease as an actor as when I got to play Mutt.

He meets Alexis at the beginning of her journey, when she was pretty wild, and he was just kind of calm and taking it all in. My favorite part of playing Mutt was my time with Alexis and my time with Annie because she's just so incredible. I loved that Mutt was part of her journey more than his own, because she becomes such an amazing woman. Not that she wasn't at the beginning, but you know when they first showed up to Schitt's Creek, the Roses were all pretty, well, there are no words to describe what the Roses were! Just to know that Mutt was a small part of that journey is an honor.

BUILDING A TOWN

*Where did the idea of the town of Schitt's Creek come
from and what does it represent?*

DANIEL LEVY: The name of the town came from a dinner
my dad had with some friends. They clearly had some wine and
thought it was very funny to come up with this theoretical town
of Schitt's Creek where you would have local businesses like
Schitt Hardware and Schitt Auto Repair. Funnily enough, when
it came to actually making the show we steered clear of those
kinds of puns. In fact, nobody in the show ever says "shit,"
s-h-i-t. That was a conscious choice we made to separate
ourselves from that joke and make the legitimacy of the town
stand on its own. As broad as the title is, we really weren't going
for that kind of humor.

When you sit down with a concept about a wealthy
family moving to a small town, I think the expected scenario
is that the town doesn't know as much as this family, and
the jokes would be at the expense of the town. For us it was
important to not go down that path. We wanted to use this
show to celebrate small towns, and to make this town way more
informed, intelligent, and accepting than our family, so that the
joke actually falls on the Roses. It was our long-term intention
that the town would act as a place where these characters
would grow and change for the better, and it was going to
be the townspeople that help them do this. It would be the
townspeople that open the Roses' eyes to goodness, kindness,
and empathy. It was an active choice to never show bigotry or
homophobia in this town and to ensure that the townspeople
were completely and totally accepting of everybody. That was
the most political we ever got on the show. To take a stand and
say we are not going to show that. We are not going to give a
voice to those kinds of conversations. This town is going to be a
beacon of light to people rather than the butt of a joke. Once we
came to that conclusion, it really informed the philosophy of the
rest of the show: that the show would continue, like the town,
to grow and change and become a safe space for people.

SCHITT'S CREEK

Where everyone fits in!

FAN ART BY DANIELLE SYLVAN

BEHIND THE SCENES
The Café Tropical and Rosebud Motel sets.
Pinewood Studios. March 31, 2017

BEHIND THE SCENES
On set with Dan and Emily in the motel lobby for
episode 213, "Happy Anniversary." May 19, 2015
(LEFT) Interior of the motel lobby. April 14, 2015

*How did you decide on the location for
the Rosebud Motel?*

BRENDAN SMITH, PRODUCTION DESIGNER: We looked at many locations for the motel, most of which didn't work out for us because of their proximity to other buildings. We were looking for something that felt very cut off from the world, because we knew this would feel like a huge contrast from the life the Roses were forced to leave behind. What we liked about the motel we eventually chose was that, although it was close to the town, it still felt rather isolated. It was pastoral, too, nestled in the fields and trees. It was also important to us that the motel had a bit of charm. It needed to be a home the Roses could grow into once they got over the shock of transitioning from being wealthy to being humble.

DANIEL LEVY: Part of the challenge when scouting for the motel was finding a perfect balance between charm and creating a level of distance from where the Roses came from. It was important to us that the town, and the experience of this family moving from their mansion into a motel, still felt warm and cozy and that it not be a complete disaster. I knew we were going to be spending a lot of time in this space, so I didn't want it to feel off-putting for the viewer. You want to create a space where the audience can feel comfortable and not be constantly cringing whenever we have to spend time in the motel.

When you look at iconic sets, the *I Love Lucy* set or any really iconic set pieces, they all have a common theme, which is that they are enjoyable places to spend time, so that was really key. We looked at a lot of motels and, unfortunately, because so few of these motels had survived, we didn't have a ton of options. But the minute we saw this one, we knew that it was hands-down the only option. It felt safe. It was tucked off the road. It was surrounded by greenery. It was aesthetically pleasing. It didn't feel seedy. It really played into the warmth of the tone of the show, and to the aesthetic that we were hoping to create.

FAN ART BY NICHOLAS HOLMAN

BEHIND THE SCENES
Exterior of the motel. Our crew wrapping up on location
after shooting episode 208, "Milk Money."
June 17, 2015

BEHIND THE SCENES
Interior of Moira and Johnny's room.
Catherine and Eugene shooting a deleted scene for
episode 401, "Dead Guy in Room 4."
April 13, 2017

There's something so retro about the interiors that invokes nostalgia for a family road trip or maybe more innocent times. Did that idea influence your vision for these spaces?

DANIEL LEVY: Totally. That idea was crucial in the set design of not only the Rosebud Motel, but Café Tropical, the Schitt House, Mutt's barn, and basically any other location we were going to be visiting regularly. For me it was about "how do you create a sense of timelessness?" For the most part, the show lives in a kind of timeless space. In the show's early days, we sat with Brendan and spent hours looking through Pinterest boards of old motels. The whole process was so fun for me and it was really important to do because you only get one shot to make a space that feels iconic. We knew this was a set that was going to live on, hopefully, for years to come if we got those seasons.

Even though there was a period aesthetic to the interiors, there was a sense of timelessness. Mid-century architecture and design is never going to go out of style, so it was really important that we rooted the interiors of our motel in and around that time period, because we knew that it was evergreen. I found a picture on Pinterest of one such motel that had a turquoise wall, and I thought that could be a really nice accent, so we decided to put that in.

Also, in terms of scale, it was important to make sure that the rooms felt small but not too small. The adjoining door between the family's rooms was a really nice touch that we ended up using in a lot of the storytelling. I'm just so thrilled with our production design team. They did such an incredible job. It really was a labor of love.

And, funnily enough, all of the research we did and the care we took in building the Rosebud Motel is what inspired us to write the storyline of Johnny's quest to revitalize roadside motels into the show. In researching where to place the Rosebud Motel, we stumbled onto information that led us to believe that the motel industry was a dying industry.

BRENDAN SMITH: For the interior sets, Dan and I looked at a lot of pictures of old motels, roadside diners, and suburban interiors, some of them very peculiar. Many of them were not places you would particularly want to stay, but they had some interesting characteristics and we found that we could grab pieces of inspiration from various references. We brought a lot of different elements together and embellished them, with the goal of making a cohesive aesthetic, but also providing emotional impact. The cement block wall behind the beds, for example, was clearly a unique decision made by someone in the past. It's honestly a bit of a shock when we and the Roses first see it, and I think it served to illustrate, without words, their rapid cultural and economic descent. With the café, too, we tried to make it feel both charming and a little odd. I think the mural always provided an interesting backdrop to lunchtime conversations.

BEHIND THE SCENES
› Interior of Café Tropical.
Eugene and Sarah rehearsing
for episode 609, "Rebound."
April 30, 2019

Appetizers

MOZZARELLA STICKS
Golden fried and served with a tasty marinara sauce. — $7.95

COCONUTTY ONION RINGS
A generous portion of rings, lightly battered with panko and macadamia nuts.
Served with BBQ sauce and Ranch dressing. — $11.49

THE TROPICAL PLATTER
A sampling of our favorite island-style appetizers. Ahi Poke, Fried Calamari,
Kalua Nachos, Spam Musubi and Macnut Onion Rings. Served with ranch
dressing, sweet & sour and teriyaki sauce. — $8.49

AHI TRIANGLES
Sushi-grade Ahi tuna on pita triangles, with green onions and white onions
mixed with soy sauce, sesame oil, Hawaiian rock salt, seaweed and crushed
red chilies. Served over freshly chopped cabbage. — $6.95

BRUSCHETTA
Olives and feta cooked in our special garlic sauce. With oregano, wine and
herbs. — $6.95

CALAMARI
Lightly battered and breaded calamari served with cocktail sauce and sweet
and sour sauce. — $8.75

Burgers & Sandwiches

Our FAMOUS Sammy's & Burgs are served with hand-cut fries unless
otherwise specified. Substitute salad or soup for $1.50, or sweet potato fries for
$1.00.

COBB SALAD SANDWICH
mixed greens & seasonal vegetables topped with blue cheese, grilled chicken,
bacon and a hard boiled egg. All on a multigrain kaiser bun. — $12.95

CHICKEN CAESER SANDWICH
Breast filet breaded and lightly seasoned with a caeser dressing, lettuce, and
tomatoes on a kaiser. Served with hand-cut fries. — $9.49

CLASSIC BURGER
Freshly ground chuck lightly seasoned with traditional garnish (toppings: natural chedar, swiss, blue, brie or feta cheese, peameal or regular bacon. — $10.95

PORTOBELLO BURGER
Topped with roasted red pepper, baby arugula and homemade basil mayo. — $8.95

CLASSIC REUBEN
Thinly sliced corned beef piled on rye bread with sauerkraut, natural Swiss
cheese, and classic Reuben dressing. — $6.95

PROP: A photograph of the original Café Tropical menu.

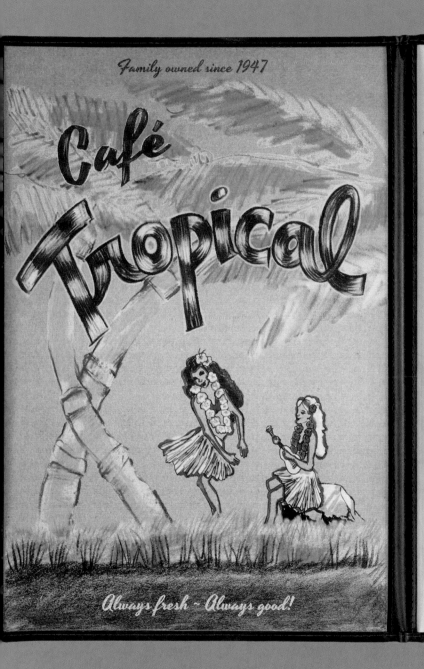

Family owned since 1947

Café Tropical

Always fresh ~ Always good!

Beverages

Free refills*

The Tropical House Blend Coffee*	$2.50	Soda water...	$2.50
Chocolate Hazlenut Coffee...	$3.50	Bottled water...	$3.50
Black Tea...	$1.75	Black Tea...	$1.75
Herbal Tea...	$1.75	Herbal Tea...	$1.75
Green tea....	$2.25	Green tea...	$2.25
Hot Chocolate	$3.15	Hot Chocolate...	$3.95
Cafe Mocha...	$3.95		
Mint Hot Chocolate...	$4.95	Soft Drinks*...	$2.95
		Iced Tea*...	$3.95
Large Shakes or Floats-	$5.95	Fruit Punch*...	$3.95
Chocolate, Strawberry,		Lemonade*...	$3.95
Vanilla, Banana, Pineapple,		Homemade Hawaiian Iced Tea*	$4.25
Pear, Coffee or the		Milk...	$1.95
Crazy Rockabilly			
(Chocolate, Peanut Butter		Small Juices-	$3.25
& Chocolate)		Guava, Passion Orange,	
		Passion Orange Guava,	
		Pineapple or Orange Juice	

Allow us to custom make your favorite drink.
Choose your favorite flavor then select a style for your cocktail.
Ask your server for suggestions!

All regular mixed drinks... $4.50

Single Custom drink ...$4.50

Double Custom drink ...$6.50

Bottled Beer

Smaut6n.....	$4.50
Ro55&Whelan.....	$5.25
Lemon4gd.....	$4.95
Smithu7pm.....	$4.75
Smooth R3d.....	$3.99
A4hhgreatoors...	$5.25
Milf2yum Light...	$4.75
Oatey R77eat...	$3.99
Smaut6n.....	$4.50
Ro55&Whelan.....	$3.99
55halmenatoors...	$4.95
Milf2yum Light...	$4.75
BruntonMauro80...	$3.99
Robertr09s Gold..	$5.25
Smu6th Smith 50....	$4.75
Mountain L4ger...	$2.75
P1askoski Lag3r..	$3.99

On Tap

Barnsley R1ch.....	$4.50
McKendy Smoo7h....	$5.25
Fisher 606 Dark.....	$4.95
Siracusa4m....	$4.75
Ba55et 99...	$3.99
Bi3rderman.....	$3.99

Wine

House White Wine	$5.75
Chardonnay	$5.95
Merlot	$6.15
Pinot Noir	$1.75
Reisling	$1.75

BRENDAN SMITH: The giant café menus were Eugene's idea. He thought it would be amusing to see the family wrestling with them when, once unfolded, they were as big as the café tables. It *was* very funny to see.

Café Tropical
Schitt's Creek
Goodwood
ON
C Breen '18

FAN ART BY CAROLYN "CHARLIE" BREEN

FAN ART BY RITA GARZA

BRENDAN SMITH: When it came to designing the interior of the Schitt House, we tried to augment their personalities. Roland's "sunken floor" was a project he was obviously very proud of. There was also the huge collection of fussy little collectibles that were lovingly curated on the shelves. These were things that were a little ridiculous, but cherished by the mayor and his wife, along with the tiny "Juliet" balcony outside the front door where she watered her flowers.

DANIEL LEVY: The Schitt house is a real house that we found that felt very much in line with Jocelyn and Roland. It was very small and cute, and it was painted a pale blue color. In those early days of creating sets you have a lot of conversations about going further to personalize the locations. We asked ourselves, "How can we go even further to make this house reflect who Roland and Jocelyn are even more than it already does?" The first thing we decided on was the sign that hangs on the entryway as you walk to their front door: "The Schitt Family Welcomes You!" The second thing was the Juliet balcony, which came out of a discussion about what Jocelyn would think was a nice design choice. If Jocelyn wanted to make pleasant and inviting improvements on her property, what would she do? She'd put in a little ground-floor Juliet balcony, which serves no purpose whatsoever, but does speak so much about the good intentions of her character. So, our design team had it made and installed, and it looked very funny and sweet. We found out later that the owners of the house really liked it and kept it. That house will forever have the gift of Jocelyn Schitt's ground-floor Juliet balcony.

BEHIND THE SCENES
Interior of the Schitt House.
(INSET) Jocelyn's figurine collection.
May 4, 2015

BEHIND THE SCENES
Interior of Mutt's barn. Annie and Tim shooting
episode 213, "Happy Anniversary."
May 22, 2015

BEHIND THE SCENES
Interior of Ted's veterinary clinic. Annie and Dustin shooting
a scene for episode 210, "Ronnie's Party."
May 21, 2015

THE BOOKS OF SCHITT'S CREEK

FAN ART BY JESSICA CRUICKSHANK
COMPILED BY @SCHITTSSHEETS

Erna Maike — SOPHISTICATION: Evaluating A Higher Aesthetic — A RARE — RHP
DAVID 105

HAROLD ZABEL. THE LAST FALLEN SOLDIER — 7rendl13ion Publishing
BOB 105

Patrick C. Lawrence — Cypher Mind
STEVIE 109

BSP — Opening Your Heart To Animals: A Guide To The Benefits Of Caring For Something Other Than Yourself. Deandra Jones
ALEXIS 109

DRIVING FORCE — MODERN BUSINESS DEVELOPMENT STRATEGIES — MILER LIPPMAN
JOHNNY 112

Waylon & Jones — Banshees on a Plane — NINA HILLMORE
STEVIE 203

WIN BIG: Entrepreneurial Strategy — Paul T. Douglas
JOHNNY 203

Waylon & Jones — BUILDING BLOCKS GEO BUSINESS IN A GLOBAL WORLD — JESSICA RUSSET
JOHNNY 211

RYLAN SONIA — Journey of a thousand miles
MOIRA 211

Nina Hillmore — ANATOMY OF A SUPERIOR AESTHETIC — RHP
DAVID 305

STERLING: The Actor's BRIDGES: Actor
MOIRA 306

60

DANIEL LEVY: Our production design team went way above and beyond with the props. You could go into the motel lobby and every pamphlet, every poster, every possible thing that you could pick up and read, was written inside and out. They didn't just design the front page of a pamphlet and then fold it and hide the rest. The same went for the books that our characters are reading throughout the six seasons. The book jackets were designed, front and back with copy, art, and evocative titles. The level of care and detail that was put in was so extraordinary and it did not go unnoticed.

DEANDRA JONES — BLOOD OPTION

A KNOCK AT THE DOOR — ERNA MAIKE — RZX2 Publishers

A HINT OF AMNESIA — SOPHIE REED

THE CARAFE OF STYLE — GINA SIMON

BIG BUSINESS PHILOSOPHY — TED CLARK — LP

SMART SYSTEMS — LP

DEIDRE NOVA — THE SNOWY NOOK

JOHNNY ROSE — FAST FORWARD TO SUCCESS — Business the Johnny Rose way — LP

MOIRA	MOIRA	MOIRA	JOHNNY	PATRICK	PATRICK	PATRICK	STEVIE
308	309	406	502	503	505	602	605

EUGENE LEVY: The discussion about what the town sign would look like came up in the writers' room, and if I'm not mistaken, it was late in the day, meaning we might have been a tad giddy. The history of the Schitt family discovering the town had to be implicit in the sign. So we thought about Roland's relatives. Perhaps his great-grandfather and great-grandmother should appear on the sign in an historical-looking backdrop. (It later became his sister when we figured out how Roland would correct the visual.) We discussed what they might be doing in the picture and the image that sent the room into hysterics was exactly what ended up on the sign.

The creation of the town sign was certainly a highlight, and it turned out to be an iconic emblem of the show. It was a scene I couldn't wait to shoot. I remember we had to keep it covered with a giant tarp between takes so that passing motorists wouldn't see it or photograph it and leak it out on social media before the episode actually aired. Shooting the scene with Rizwan was even more fun to shoot than it was to write. And the later scene with Chris easily takes first prize in having the saltiest dialogue of any in our six seasons. Screaming those lines at Roland on the soft shoulder of a rural Ontario highway was exhilarating for me because, as funny as they read on paper, they sounded even funnier coming out of my mouth.

RIZWAN MANJI: The first time I actually spoke the words of Ray was at a table read for the episode "Don't Worry, It's His Sister," which is the scene with Eugene at the sign. I was very nervous and thinking, "I don't know. It's written on the page, but there's so many different ways you can do it." But I think in the table read you just make a choice, and afterward I asked Dan, and he said, "No, no, do it like that, I loved it!" And I was like, "Okay!" In that episode, the whole situation was a little annoying—for Johnny and the audience—because Ray wasn't getting it, he was sort of naïve, he doesn't get why the sign isn't appropriate. But that was part of it—it captures the intrusion of the Roses on the optimism of the town, a theme that developed through the seasons. There was definitely a flavor of that in the beginning. It's such an iconic scene and it's one of my favorite moments.

BEHIND THE SCENES
Schitt's Creek town sign. Episode 103,
"Don't Worry, It's His Sister."

"The world is falling apart around us, John.
And I'm dying inside."

MOIRA ROSE

season

1

SUNLESS BRONZER

FAN ART BY
JESSICA CRUICKSHANK

SEASON ONE

Bad Parents

Written by
Kevin White

Directed by
Jerry Ciccoritti

Johnny and Moira come to the stunning realization that they might be terrible parents. David tries to sell some of his clothes for extra cash and Alexis investigates Mutt's mysterious relationship with the mayor's wife.

101

Our Cup Runneth Over

Written by
Daniel Levy

Directed by
Jerry Ciccoritti

After losing their fortune, the Rose family must relocate to their last remaining asset, a small town called Schitt's Creek that Johnny once bought as a joke. They move into the motel, where they meet the town's mayor, Roland Schitt, and begin their new life that, unbeknownst to anyone, will change them and the town forever.

102

The Drip

Written by
Chris Pozzebon

Directed by
Jerry Ciccoritti

After Johnny wakes up soaking wet from a leak in the ceiling, he decides that he must sell the town, but he and Moira soon discover that's easier said than done. Meanwhile, David and Alexis check out the local nightlife at a tailgate party. Alexis looks for a new boyfriend, while David gets to know Stevie, the girl that runs the motel.

103

Don't Worry, It's His Sister

Written by
Michael Short

Directed by
Paul Fox

Johnny is shocked by the town sign and plans to take it down, only to discover its meaning to Roland. Alexis runs into Mutt, the guy she made out with the night before, while David is faced with the near-impossible task of finding a job. Moira's bad day turns around when she meets Jocelyn at the café.

105

The Cabin

Written by
Amanda Walsh

Directed by
Paul Fox

Looking for privacy, Johnny and Moira take up Roland's offer to go to his cabin to rekindle their romance. With their parents away, Alexis convinces David to host a quiet game night, but secretly plans to turn the event into an all-out rager. The night falls apart when David and Alexis do what they do best—fight with each other.

106

Wine and Roses

Written by
Kevin White

Directed by
Jerry Ciccoritti

Moira is offered her first acting role in years as the spokesperson for a local fruit winery. Johnny tries to help relaunch her career. Meanwhile, David is suffering from a mysterious illness and must visit the only doctor in town, the local vet. Alexis finds that her feelings for Mutt are becoming uncomfortably strong.

107

Turkey Shoot

Written by
Daniel Levy and
Michael Grassi

Directed by
Paul Fox

David agrees to attend the annual turkey shoot with Stevie. Meanwhile, Moira's stress level is through the roof, so Jocelyn takes her for a spa day in Elmdale. Things go badly when she ends up coming home looking just like Jocelyn. Alexis accepts a date with Ted.

108
Allez-Vous

Written by
Chris Pozzebon

Directed by
Paul Fox

Moira and David try to earn money by selling cosmetics to the local townsfolk, while Johnny heads to Elmdale in hopes of collecting unemployment insurance. Alexis thinks her new boyfriend, Ted, is too nice and tries to turn him into someone her family will respect.

109
Carl's Funeral

Written by
Kevin White

Directed by
Jerry Ciccoritti

Johnny reluctantly agrees to speak at the funeral of Bob's brother, a man he doesn't even know. Ted's love of animals is getting in the way of Alexis's love life. Meanwhile, David and Stevie get up close and personal, crossing the line from friends to friends with benefits.

110
Honeymoon

Written by
Daniel Levy

Directed by
Jerry Ciccoritti

After they spend a night together, David and Stevie's relationship seems to be more than what they both bargained for. Johnny and Moira invite themselves to Roland and Jocelyn's luau. Hoping to show off their perfect relationship, Alexis and Ted throw a couple's dinner party, but things go south when Alexis's relationship with Mutt is questioned.

111
Little Sister

Written by
Michael Short

Directed by
Paul Fox

Moira's estranged sister, Deedee, pays an unexpected visit. David steps out of his comfort zone by trying to help one of Jocelyn's students who's having a hard time fitting in. Alexis meddles in Mutt's relationship with Twyla by giving her some unsolicited advice.

112
Surprise Party

Written by
Chris Pozzebon

Directed by
Paul Fox

Johnny tries to arrange a surprise birthday party for Moira. Things backfire when Moira, unwittingly, takes over the planning of her own event and David tries to do damage control. Alexis and Johnny have some father-daughter time when they visit Elmdale to pick up the birthday cake.

113
Town for Sale

Written by
Daniel Levy and
Kevin White

Directed by Jerry Ciccoritti

Johnny finds a potential buyer for the town. All he needs now is the buyer's signature on the deed. Meanwhile, David and Alexis discover they may have become more attached to Schitt's Creek than they ever thought possible.

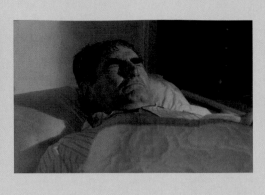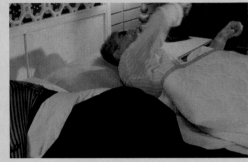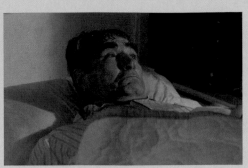

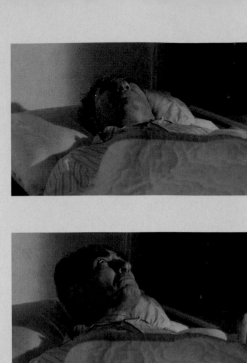

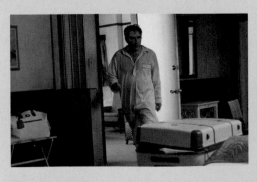

Behind the Episode

Johnny and the drip.

EUGENE LEVY: The drip scene in episode 102 is just one example of how much fun my son had writing a scene at my expense. I vividly remember the idea for this scene coming up in the writers' room and what a positive response it got, particularly from one Daniel Levy. Daniel knows I'm particular about my hair. It's not due to vanity so much as it is the fact that it's a time-consuming process to get my hair to look as good as I would like. If you were born with this hair, you would understand. Better yet, if my son had been born with it, this scene would never have gotten off the ground.

Because this was Johnny and Moira's first morning in the motel—the first morning of their new nightmare—the idea of Johnny waking up to discover a leaking pipe above his bed that had been dripping on him all night, soaking his hair and his nightshirt, was a funny scenario and a good idea. There was no denying that. So my professional self rose to the occasion, and I agreed to do it. Unkempt hair be damned.

They sprayed me down with water before the scene. I checked myself in the mirror and thought, "Hair doesn't look too bad. I can live with that." And then I heard a voice coming from off the set: "I think it could be more wet!" The voice belonged to my son. "The joke will play if it's more wet. You have to be drenched," he said.

Johnny's reaction to the leak was to become panicked and extremely angry at his new surroundings, so the situation I was experiencing on set really lent itself to the moment. But, the truth is, I got a kick out of the delight Daniel was taking in watching me suffer. It was a funny scene and an appropriate introduction for the Roses to their new home, the Schitt's Creek Motel.

DANIEL LEVY: The great thing about working with your family as a writer is that you know their sensitive spots. My dad is at his most vulnerable when it comes to his hair. He spends a lot of time on it, he's very protective of it, and he doesn't want people touching it. So, to write this scene for Johnny where he wakes up to a wet, dirty leak in the ceiling that's dripped on his head all night felt like, on a personal level, something that I would really love to see my dad react to. I also knew what he would give us as an actor, because in those moments Eugene and Johnny Rose become the same person. It was fun for me to get to push his buttons as a human and as an actor. This ended up being one of my favorite scenes. As his son, when I watch this scene, I see my dad because he is so close to his character and his character is so close to him in that moment. There ended up being several scenes written over the course of the six seasons that were funny little jabs between father and son.

The tailgate party.

ANNIE MURPHY: The tailgate party was a very fun night, and nothing says summer like teetering around a cow field in four-inch stilettos! I honestly don't remember if it was the tailgate party or if it was our first steamy kiss in the barn, but for whatever reason Tim's beard wasn't really properly dyed in that first season. I want to say it was just covered with borderline shoe polish to make it look darker. I remember being so nervous because it was one of my first on-screen kisses, and I remember going in and kissing Tim and pulling away, and Tim's face just had this look of pure terror on it. And I was like, "What have I done?" Then someone came in and held up a mirror, and I saw that I had black ink all over three-quarters of my face. It was truly everywhere.

TIM ROZON: It takes twenty-one days to grow the official Mutt beard that everybody likes. And I know this because that's how long it took after I shaved to grow it back for the scenes that we still had to shoot. For twenty-one days I sat around growing a beard, waiting to get back to work. During this time the incredible Eugene Levy and I became friends because we both have a mutual love of the Toronto Blue Jays. So, while I was growing my beard, he took me to a couple of Jays games. Front-row Jays games with Eugene was just amazing. José Bautista and all the guys would come over and say hi to Eugene. I'll never forget that.

Behind the Episode

104 **BAD PARENTS**

Ronnie and the Roses.

KAREN ROBINSON: I think this scene from "Bad Parents" may have been the first scene that I shot. I remember the nerves. Thank Christ I was sitting down, because I'm not sure my knees would've held me up. In this scene Ronnie asks Alexis, "So, what's your deal, you're pretty. What's that like?" I spent a lot of my younger years wondering what pretty people's lives were like, so that question came from a very real place, and, besides, Annie really is *beautiful*.

Ronnie's relationship with Alexis and the Roses definitely evolved over time. I think the more Ronnie likes you, the more she'll let you into her orbit. Once you're there, you'll be treated to an even closer look at her trademark scowl. The Roses all got a healthy dose of that.

Behind the Episode

106   WINE AND ROSES

Herb Ertlinger's fruit wine.

CATHERINE O'HARA: Any chance for Moira to show off was a chance for me to be nervous. But even Moira was so off her game at this point that she needed (more than) a few drinks to get through the Herb Ertlinger commercial shoot. I love the challenge of playing drunk. Drunk people not only rarely admit they're drunk, they often have all the confidence in the world. It's quite freeing to play that.

Honestly, I was nervous again at the end of the scene, improvising ridiculous versions of Herb's name.

DANIEL LEVY: Catherine has such a sharp idea of who Moira is and who she isn't. For us it's been really great to sit back and watch her bring Moira to life in ways that we had never even imagined. She has brought such complexity and depth and dimension to every character that she's played. She can go from drama to comedy in a heartbeat and make every note true and real and funny and rich and powerful.

This scene was a beautiful combination of both script and ad-libbing. Nobody plays drunk like Catherine. There's such a reality to her drunkenness. It doesn't feel performative. It feels lived-in. As soon as I saw the first take, I knew not only were we going to have a really funny scene, but that this scene was going to be one that would come to define our show. It was so early in the season, so to see something like that was such a confidence builder for all of us.

Seeing that clip being shared all over the internet became one of the first barometers of our success. It really was one of the first water-cooler moments for us and it became the gold standard that pushed us to quest after that next iconic scene for Catherine.

I don't even think she did that many takes. And yes, everything that happened at the end of that monologue, the sort of messy run of names, that was all Catherine.

BEHIND THE SCENES
In between takes with Catherine on location shooting *the* wine commercial in episode 106, "Wine and Roses."
June 25, 2014

FAN ART BY CHRIS ABLES

Schitt's Creek - 106 - X2WHITE - 12 June 2014 36.

TAG

22 HERB ERTLINGER WINERY PROMOTIONAL VIDEO 22

Walking amid the fruit trees and shrubs, Moira, being shot with an abundance of gauze on the lens, speaks confidently and directly to camera.

You can barely tell she's loaded.

MOIRA

In the lee of a picturesque ridge, lies a small unpretentious winery. One that pampers its fruit like its own babies. Hi, I'm Moira Rose, and if you love fruit wine as much as I do, then you'll appreciate the craftsmanship and quality of a local vintner who brings to life the fruity goodness of his Oak Chardonnay and dazzling apple-lime tones to his award-winning Riesling Fume. So come taste the difference good fruit can make in your wine. You'll remember the experience. And you'll remember the name - Herb... Ertlinnnng... Bbbertling... her-BERT-ling... herbert-LING-er... harbartlinger... habart, herb art ling art er...

END OF SHOW

BEHIND THE SCENES

Original script for "Wine and Roses."

Behind the Episode

107 TURKEY SHOOT

"Turkey virgin!"

KAREN ROBINSON: "Turkey Shoot" was the first moment where we see how Ronnie fits into her community. I had a real sense of her belonging to the town in that episode, and I think her willingness to initiate David into the fold was a really lovely and caring moment. I guess hunting brings out Ronnie's soft side! That part where I coach David on how to hold a rifle is on my demo reel, and there it will stay for as long as possible.

EMILY HAMPSHIRE: I love the early days of David and Stevie's relationship where she takes such pleasure in fucking with him. When I think of "Turkey Shoot," I immediately think of Dan in that hat! It had this floppy camo-cutout leaf that kept falling onto his forehead, and he kept trying to casually blow it out of his line of vision like some French girl whose curtain bangs fell over one eye. I also still find myself stealing the line "I'm at one with nature" for my real life, because I'm not. I'm what Roland would call an "indoorsy" kind of person.

DANIEL LEVY: I always loved shooting on location. It brought a whole new level of authenticity to the story we were telling, to be outside of our sets. And I also loved the big group scenes. I loved writing them and I loved acting in them.

This scene was shot very early in our run and we were still getting to know each other. So, to spend a day with Karen, John, Emily, and Chris was really a bonding experience for all of us. There's also something inherently funny in seeing everyone show up on sct in full hunting apparel, knowing who we all are in real life and how far it was from our realities. It turned out to be a very funny scene and they made me laugh through the whole shoot.

Behind the Episode

Alexis meets Ted.

DUSTIN MILLIGAN: I loved every minute of working with Annie. We became such good friends over the course of our six seasons together. From our very first day on set together, in this scene when Ted meets Alexis in the café, I immediately felt comfortable with her. I was nervous going in, but then seeing Annie drop so effortlessly into the character of Alexis, who is so hilariously self-absorbed, really put me at ease. From that moment on, I knew we would be in perfect sync with each other. It's a strange thing when you find someone you click with instantly, someone you know you can trust through the wobbly parts of a scene that we all experience sometimes. But, as soon as they called "action," I knew I'd found my partner.

ANNIE MURPHY: This may have been Dustin's first day on set. I remember knowing immediately that we were going to be trouble together, because we kept making each other crack up, and that was a constant theme throughout the six years that we worked together. It was a great feeling to know: Okay, I'm going to be comfortable with this person. We're going to have a good time. I'm going to go in every day and act with a dear friend. That's such a wonderful feeling to have.

I just watched this scene again recently. I was so struck by the confidence, and also the fake coquettishness that Alexis puts on. It's so funny to me how Alexis is one hundred percent certain that she is beyond the most attractive woman in town, but that she also has the presence to add just a sprinkle of humble into the mix. I also really love what the writers did with bringing this scene back in the final moments between Ted and Alexis in season six. In the original scene, Alexis says, "I'm sure there's another *girl* somewhere." And then in the final scene, she says, "I'm sure there's another *woman* somewhere." I think that's such a wonderful example of the growth that she's gone through over the years.

DANIEL LEVY: This scene in the café, when Alexis first meets Ted, was such a fun scene to shoot. In season one you're seeing Alexis in a very different light than you see her in later seasons, so there was fun to be had around her extreme level of self-absorption in the early episodes.

We had established Mutt as the bad boy, and the conversation in the writers' room was about who is the type of person Alexis would be least attracted to? We realized she historically had always gone after the bad guys. She was always enamored with men who lived life on the edge. So, we

wanted to introduce a character for her as a potential love interest that was the polar opposite of that. Someone who was self-reliant, self-sufficient, had a good job, cared about what he did, had his life together, but wasn't in any way edgy—had absolutely no edge—but was smitten with her from day one. That felt like a really nice angel to put on her other shoulder, considering Mutt was the proverbial devil.

We knew then that we were eventually going to have her realize that she doesn't have to chase the bad guys. She deserves a good guy. She deserves a guy who will love her unconditionally and respect her own desires and professional ideas and ambitions. And we knew it was going to be a very slow burn. I think this first scene really laid that groundwork well. Annie did such a great job of playing that dialogue. "I'm sure there's another girl somewhere" was a line that I loved on paper and then adored when I saw it on screen. Then, of course, we called back to that scene in the last season in the episode when Ted and Alexis break up. It was all kind of premeditated, and we were just very fortunate to have really skilled actors take those words and make them into something really magical.

Behind the Episode

The very first "Ew, David."

ANNIE MURPHY: The "Allez-Vous" episode is the first time Alexis said the phrase "Ew, David." What blows my mind is I think I only said, "Ew, David" two or three times in the entire series, which is staggering if you think about the phenomenon that it has become. I remember I saw it on paper and it just felt so right. I loved the sound of it. I also loved the impact it had on Dan as David. I remember after the first time Alexis said, "Ew, David," I started adding "David" onto as many things as I possibly could. Like "Ugh, David" or "Burn, David." The inflection was always there but the actual words "Ew, David" are in the show way less than you might imagine.

I recently learned that someone put out a map of North America that shows all of the states and provinces that have an "Ew, David" license plate. It's quite overwhelming. It's like the majority of North America! And poor Dan. Apparently people scream, "Ew, David" at him on the street and from car windows all the time. That can't always feel good.

BEHIND THE SCENES

Thank you to everyone who contributed a photograph of your EWDAVID license plate!

ALABAMA
Ashleigh Walker

SASKATCHEWAN
Lacey Fraser

MINNESOTA
Kari Robak

ILLINOIS
Laura A. Markun

KANSAS
Katie Coriell

ARIZONA
Lawrence R. Vigil Jr.

KENTUCKY
Jenn Moses

SOUTH CAROLINA
Chad Hefty

NEBRASKA
Rob Tualaulelei

NORTH CAROLINA
Laura Ziel

NEW JERSEY
Kelly (Sawyer) Fleming

WYOMING
Jeanne Core

MICHIGAN
Brittney Kinney

COLORADO
David Ethridge

MARYLAND
Kelly Foy

INDIANA
Melody Hawkins

VIRGINIA
Jennifer Ludovici

CALIFORNIA
Huntley Woods

ALBERTA
Jennifer Carson

WISCONSIN
Rachel Schroepfer

MANITOBA
Traci Lea Wright

ONTARIO
Heidi Adams

NOVA SCOTIA
Louise Downs

ALASKA
Chelsea Robinson

NEW YORK
Emily Schwartz

FLORIDA
Michael Decying

MAINE
Dylan M. Guy Jr.

NORTH DAKOTA
Leah Riveland-Foster

PENNSYLVANIA
Julianna Morris

OKLAHOMA
@itssydneylouise

UTAH
Aryn Nelson

CONNECTICUT
Sarah Vazquez

OHIO
Jason Gray

WEST VIRGINIA
Ashley Glock

GEORGIA
Marina Brenke

IOWA
Hannah Bartel

RHODE ISLAND
Gianna C. DeLuca

NEVADA
Sam Wong

MASSACHUSETTS
Amanda Greene

MISSOURI
DJ Wilke

IDAHO
Rebekah Harvey

OREGON
Helen Salley

Behind the Episode

"Oh, Danny boy!"

DANIEL LEVY: This scene is a prime example of the brilliance of my dad and Catherine O'Hara, and the kind of intangible chemistry they have that is so rare to see on screen. We didn't know how Moira was going to perform "Danny Boy," but we were all pleasantly surprised when we got on set and watched her do it. You can't really write that moment. You can only set it up to be launched by really great actors. My dad holding the sandwich in between bites to hear if she would keep going or not and then she does, and then he eats the sandwich again, is why he is now an Emmy-winning actor.

The Johnny-Moira relationship was really informed by Catherine and my dad. It was very important to them that they not portray a bickering couple using a tragic circumstance to separate from each other, because that's the expected thing to do. They really wanted to show a successful couple that, despite their circumstance, only continued to support each other and didn't crack under the pressure; didn't turn on each other at all. Instead, they used the tragedy of their lives to express their love and support for each other in deeper and more meaningful ways.

Behind the Episode

"I like the wine and not the label."

EMILY HAMPSHIRE: The "wine not the label" scene *literally* changed my life, but I didn't even realize it when we were shooting. We get so many messages about how the show has changed people's lives, but we actors weren't immune to that "*Schitt's Creek* effect." This show didn't just change my career, it changed my personal life, too.

Before *Schitt's Creek* I thought I was super open-minded and presumably knowledgeable when it came to all things LGBTQIA+. I've been in the entertainment industry since I was eleven years old and all my friends were gay men. But I remember when we were shooting this scene about wine as a metaphor for David's pansexuality, I had to ask Dan what it meant. I'd never heard the word "pansexual" before, and while I was always so comfortable with other people's sexuality, I'd never really thought about my own.

A few years later, I saw comments from people discussing and debating my sexuality after a relationship I was in had become public. Suddenly I felt like I had to define this thing about me that had always been, well . . . complicated. I remember asking Dan at one point, "What am I? I just fall for a person—for their vibe—and I genuinely don't even think about their gender. I'm either attracted to them or I'm not, based on kind of everything *but* gender." And Dan was like, "Do you not watch our show!? You're pan!"

What I love most about this scene now is how unfazed and accepting Stevie is. I think Stevie's attitude toward David's sexuality was an early example of how the people of Schitt's Creek would never be homophobic and always be accepting of people's differences.

DANIEL LEVY: The "wine not the label" scene was a tricky one to write, because I didn't want it to feel heavy-handed and I didn't want it to feel like we were teaching people. It was really important to me that the concept of pansexuality be expressed with the same kind of casual confidence that David carried himself with. He saw his queerness as nothing but just who he was. That really was an overarching philosophy for me in the show. I never wanted to cater to people who didn't understand. There are shows that tackle the tragic side of the LGBTQIA+ community. It was always my goal to show nothing but light. Part of that is presenting things as they are without batting an eye.

It also spoke to a larger conversation that was quite deliberate, which was the enigma of David Rose. We knew that people would be asking questions because David wasn't easy to read. And if he *was* easy to read, there would be an assumption that he was gay. When David first kissed Stevie, we knew the audience would think, "Wait a minute. Is he not . . . ?" It was really important for me to play on that all-too-common assumption of who people are based on how they present themselves. The hope was that this moment would illuminate our own biases and reflexes when it comes to jumping to conclusions about other people.

To play Stevie and David's relationship out as we did, and then to introduce Jake into the mix, served to further expand the conversation that I think we need to have with ourselves about how we should be more careful about judging people.

Schitt's Creek - 110 - GOLD - 18 June 2014 16

ACT TWO

9 INT. GENERAL STORE - DAY 9

David and Stevie are picking out a wine to bring for dinner.

DAVID
Detroit makes wine?

STEVIE
I usually pick the one with the
nicest label.

DAVID
You know who else does that?

STEVIE
Who?

DAVID
The contestants on The Bachelor.

STEVIE
Just to be clear. I'm a red wine
drinker.

DAVID
That's fine.

STEVIE
Okay. Cool. But, like, I only drink
red wine.

DAVID
Okay.

STEVIE
And up until last night I was under
the impression that you might
also... only drink red wine. But I
guess I was wrong.

DAVID
I see where you're going with this.
And you're not wrong. I do drink
red wine. But I also drink white.

STEVIE
Okay...

(CONTINUED)

BEHIND THE SCENES
Original script for "Honeymoon."

9   CONTINUED: 9

                         DAVID
                    I've also enjoyed the occasional
                    Rose.

                         STEVIE
                    Okay. So, you're just really open
                    to all wines.

                         DAVID
                    I'm into the wine. Not the label.
                    Does that make sense?

                         STEVIE
                    Yes. It does. Well, this is new for
                    me. I've never been with such an
                    open minded wine drinker. So, I
                    guess as long as you didn't roll
                    over and cry yourself to sleep with
                    regret, then we're good.

                         DAVID
                         (sarcastically)
                    Oh no, I absolutely did that. Wept
                    for hours. In the dark.

        They share a laugh. Things seem to have normalized.

10   OMITTED   10

BEHIND THE SCENES
Eugene and Chris on location for episode 110 "Honeymoon."
June 18, 2014

ROLAND My son lives in a barn in the woods, by choice! He could be the next mayor of this town if he wanted it.

JOHNNY My son is "pansexual."

ROLAND Mm-hmm. I've heard of that. I know what that is, that's uh . . . that cookware fetish.

JOHNNY No.

ROLAND Mm-hmm!

JOHNNY No, no.

ROLAND No, I read about that!

JOHNNY No, he loves everyone, men, women, women who become men, men who become women. I'm his father, and I always wanted his life to be easy. But you know, just pick one gender, and maybe, maybe everything would've been less . . . confusing.

ROLAND Well, you know, Johnny, when it comes to matters of the heart, we can't tell our kids who to love. Who said that?

JOHNNY You did.

ROLAND When?

JOHNNY You just said it now!

ROLAND When?

JOHNNY Now, right this second, you just said it. And you're right, you can't tell them. And I'm fine with that.

In conversation with

DANIEL LEVY *and*
EMILY HAMPSHIRE

*On David and Stevie's special
"friendlationship."*

DL   One of my favorite elements
of the show has always been the
relationship between Stevie and
David. From the very first moment
they meet in the motel office it's a
relationship that's so complicated
and yet so easy. They shouldn't be
friends, yet they are.

EH   I love David and Stevie's
"friendlationship," as I call it. It's
the kind of relationship I've never
seen on TV, but that I have in real
life. You're not together as a couple,
but you're more than friends.
You're like kindred spirit animals.

DL   I think the reason our
audience has found so much
humor and joy in the Stevie-David
dynamic is that Stevie and David
care so much about each other, but
they'll never tell each other how
they feel. It's just implied.

EH   I also think they saw
themselves in each other. From
the moment they met, I think they
both clocked this internal witty
intelligence and sarcasm they
shared. You know that amazing
feeling when you find somebody
that finally gets your sarcasm
without you having to explain it?
There's this kind of internal sigh
of "Oh my god, somebody I don't
have to dumb it down for and say,
I'm just joking." You can really
say it straight like, "Yeah, the
Hammam spa is just down
the hall."

DL   I feel like deep down
they know that there's a deep
connection, but they never have
to talk about it.

BEHIND THE SCENES
Emily and Dan on set for episode 112 "Surprise Party."
April 30, 2014

94

Behind the Episode

"We're finally getting out!"

EUGENE LEVY: I laughed when I read the opening scene of the season one finale, because I knew my son had another good laugh at my expense when he wrote it. He knows his father is not a runner. And still, Daniel wrote a scene that had Johnny running across town, in a full suit and dress shoes, until he damn near collapses with exhaustion when he finally reaches the motel to tell the family the good news—that we had a buyer for the town and we are finally getting out.

The joke became less funny the closer I got to shooting the scene, when the realization hit me that I actually had to *do the running*. When I was asked by production if I wanted a stunt man to do the running for me, I was seized by the shock that there was a perception that I might be too old to run! I had to nip that perception in the bud. And so, I ran. And ran. And I surprised myself by how good I felt. And how much better I would have felt had I been running in sneakers.

Behind the Episode

113 TOWN FOR SALE

"I'd kill for a good coma right now."

EUGENE LEVY: The entirety of season one, for the audience and for the Roses, was meant to convey this family's horror and unhappiness with their new life in Schitt's Creek. For Johnny, his job was crystal clear: to figure a way out for his family and to keep their spirits up. Moira's attitude was "never give up." She believed firmly that the Rose family exodus from Schitt's Creek would happen; it was only a matter of time. Alexis coped with her new situation by resolving herself to the fact that life goes on, so you should make the most of it. David just needed to make it through his feeling of desolation without losing his sanity.

As season one ends and a prospective buyer comes in to buy the town, it's great news for the Roses. They were finally leaving this podunk town! But when the deal falls through, the stark realization hits them: their nightmare is far from over. They will have to learn to take things day by day and accept their life as it is. And they will have to rely on the good people of Schitt's Creek to help them do it.

Our expectation for them in season two and beyond is that they will begin to make those adjustments. They may never get back to life as they knew it, so learning to become citizens of Schitt's Creek will be the order of the day.

BEHIND THE SCENES
On set with the Rose family
for the season one finale.
May 27, 2014

"I mean, would it kill someone
to plant a few peonies?"

MOIRA ROSE

season

2

FAN ART BY JESSICA CRUICKSHANK

SEASON TWO

201
Finding David

Written by
Daniel Levy

Directed by
Jerry Ciccoritti

The Roses finally go in search of David and Moira's crocodile bag, which has been missing for several days. Alexis must make a difficult choice between Ted and Mutt, despite technically being engaged to Ted. Luckily, she's able to delay her decision when David is found in the most unlikely of places.

202
Family Dinner

Written by
David West Read

Directed by
Jerry Ciccoritti

Moira decides to cook dinner for the family and enlists David's help in making her mother's enchiladas. Johnny scopes out an office for his business. Alexis finally comes clean with Ted about their engagement.

203
Jazzagals

Written by
Michael Short

Directed by
Paul Fox

Moira attempts to join the Jazzagals, the town's a cappella group led by Jocelyn. David plans to build a cedar box for his moth-ridden knits, while Alexis enjoys the first heady days of her relationship with Mutt. Johnny discovers that working out of Bob's garage requires him to be a little more hands-on than he'd hoped.

204
Estate Sale

Written by
Teresa Pavlinek

Directed by
Jerry Ciccoritti

Johnny and Moira find a brand-new mattress at an estate sale but are outbid for it by Jocelyn. Mutt surprises Alexis with a bike and she's less than thrilled with the gift. Meanwhile, Roland asks David to help him shop for a special gift for Jocelyn.

205
Bob's Bagels

Written by
Chris Pozzebon
and Daniel Levy

Directed by
Paul Fox

In an attempt to show off his business acumen, Johnny pitches a business idea that Bob takes too seriously. David goes for an interview at the Blouse Barn, while Moira reluctantly cares for an ailing Alexis.

206
Moira vs. Town Council

Written by
Daniel Levy

Directed by
Jerry Ciccoritti

Fed up with her town looking like a garbage heap, Moira tries to effect change by voicing her complaints to the Town Council. Alexis's relationship is thrown into jeopardy when Mutt makes the rash decision to update his look. David takes full advantage of his company credit card and it's up to Johnny to reel him in before it's too late.

207
The Candidate

Written by
Kevin White

Directed by
Paul Fox

Johnny contemplates running for Town Council, but Moira puts a damper on his campaign before it's even started. David and Stevie test their newfound friendship by trying to pick up strangers at a bar, while Alexis struggles to come to terms with her status as "single."

208
Milk Money

Written by
Michael Short

Directed by
Paul Fox

In the hopes of making some quick money, Johnny enters the raw milk business, but things quickly take a turn for the worse when Alexis is left in charge of ordering the supply. Moira, feeling disconnected from the voting public, attempts to bond with some of the locals. Meanwhile, David offers style advice to her competition, without fully considering the consequences.

209
Moira's Nudes

Written by
David West Read

Directed by
Jerry Ciccoritti

Moira worries that salacious photos from her past will surface on the internet and jeopardize her campaign. Johnny swallows his pride in order to ask for financial help. Alexis becomes gainfully and surprisingly employed.

210
Ronnie's Party

Written by
Matt Kippen

Directed by
Paul Fox

Seeking voters for her election bid, Moira manages to tee up a meeting with a "key demographic." Johnny tags along and quickly realizes that Moira may have misread the room. Alexis's new job proves to be harder than she thought it would be. And David's boss saddles him with his biggest responsibility yet: her 14-year-old stepdaughter.

211
The Motel Guest

Written by
Kevin White

Directed by
Jerry Ciccoritti

Johnny and Moira have to deal with a surprise motel guest, who turns out to be Roland, while Alexis, flush with money from her new job, asks David to go apartment hunting with her.

212
Lawn Signs

Written by
Kevin White

Directed by
Jerry Ciccoritti

When some of Moira's campaign signs mysteriously disappear, Johnny immediately accuses Roland of foul play. David suddenly finds himself unemployed when the Blouse Barn becomes entangled in a legal dispute. With the help of Alexis, he turns the situation into a financial windfall for his boss and for himself.

213
Happy Anniversary

Written by
Daniel Levy

Directed by
Paul Fox

To celebrate their anniversary, Johnny and Moira go out to the finest restaurant in Elmdale. The night takes an unexpected turn when they bump into friends from their previous life. Meanwhile David and Alexis hit Mutt's barn party, where David and Stevie compete for the same guy and Alexis finally accepts the end of her relationship with Mutt.

FPS: 23.976 SHUTTER: 180° FI: 800 WB: 5600°K LUT: REC 709
-3cc

B116 SCENE 12D TAKE 2 LENS: 65
STOP 8

SCHITT'S DIR: JERRY CICCORITTI FILTER:
CREEK DP: GERALD PACKER csc SND 1
SEASON 2 EPS: 1 DATE: ND 2

Behind the Episode

On costume and character.

DANIEL LEVY: I have long admired the necessity of costume in film and television. When it's used properly it can speak volumes, and not just about a character. It can indicate theme, it can set tone; there's just so much that can be done within the world of costuming that doesn't involve exposition or unnecessary dialogue. My biggest pet peeve is listening to characters tell me who they are, what they like, and what they don't. The way people dress says so much about who they are.

When it came to deciding on the aesthetic for each of our characters, we took the same approach that we took for the show itself. We wanted their aesthetic to live in as timeless a world as we could possibly create. When I think about timeless TV, what really stands out to me are characters that have an iconic look. Characters that you would want to dress up as for Halloween. Those characters tend to have a pretty standard uniform. I think of Bart Simpson, for example, or *Married With Children*. The way those characters dress never changes, and yet you never tire of those looks.

David's aesthetic, in particular, was a really interesting story for me. Through his clothes you can instantly see his connection to Moira without us ever having to write anything about it. The idea that David would look to Moira for his aesthetic—this very avant-garde, fashion-forward, highly directional, black-and-white sartorial voice that Moira has—and then emulate it for himself as a way to be close to her felt really powerful. I knew from day one that David would also be in black and white and that his aesthetic would mirror Moira's.

I also wanted his sartorial choices to reflect his sexuality and never conform to any gender or sexual box. We played with Rick Owens a lot, Neil Barrett, Dries Van Noten, all of these designers that have lived outside the box. Rick Owens, in particular, has really played with creating a gender-nonconforming voice for his clothing. And that set a tone for David. In the very first look that we see from him, when he arrives at the motel, he's wearing a Rick Owens jacket that I had actually bought for myself many years prior. We worked with long t-shirts and played with proportion and the kilts and skirts that he would wear over the pants. The way he chose to express himself was, on the one hand all over the place, but on the other hand very specific. And, when he was going through a major moment in his life, we tried to make sure that his clothes spoke to that moment.

BEHIND THE SCENES
Dan and Lucy Earle on location for "Finding David."
June 4, 2015

Behind the Episode

201 FINDING DAVID

Finishing an iconic look.

DEBRA HANSON, COSTUME DESIGNER: For the scene in "Finding David," I knew that Dan would be wearing the outlandish Helmut Lang sweater. It's an amazing piece—just so perfect and bizarre. I also knew in this episode Moira would be looking for her son (and her crocodile bag) against the backdrop of the farm and the Amish in their traditionally plain style of dress. I thought, Moira and David need to work visually as a mother and son pairing. There was also the very strong concept of them being out in nature. David in his sweater looked like a pony in the field, so I wanted Moira to be his visual counterpart in nature.

We already had the Balenciaga tights. Those had been sitting on my table for quite some time. So, we said, "Let's start with those." Dan said, "Let's do them with the miniskirt." So, we had the look, but we didn't have anything for Moira's head and that really bothered me. We needed a visual balance to the hood on David's sweater.

I did a lot of millinery when I was at the National Theater School, so I got a hat form and started to play with putting feathers on it. Then, I took some grosgrain ribbon that we found and wrapped it around the hat form and secured it with a buckle I had in my kit. We looked it over and thought, "It needs one more step." So, I asked, "Can we find some bigger feathers? Can you find me a pheasant? She's going to the country!" So, we found those big feathers and stuck them in her cap and sent it off to Dan, Catherine, and Ana Sorys, our hairstylist, to see what they thought. We all just fell off our chairs. It looked perfect. Catherine could really wear it because it was all about the balance with the rest of her look, and in concert with David's look. I have to tell you, it was my favorite costume.

BEHIND THE SCENES
Catherine (in Moira's iconic look for "Finding David") filming with Eugene on location.
June 4, 2015

BEHIND THE SCENES
Taking a break for some fun and refreshments on location for "Finding David."
June 4, 2015

FAN ART BY JUSTIN TEODORO

In conversation with

DEBRA HANSON, DANIEL LEVY,

and CATHERINE O'HARA

On building an aesthetic for Moira Rose.

DEBRA HANSON: Catherine had the idea of using Daphne Guinness, the larger-than-life British socialite and fashion icon, as her inspiration for Moira's look. Strangely enough, I had been thinking along the same lines and so had Dan. We both knew exactly what Catherine was talking about, because Daphne Guinness is eccentric, but she's also very strong, intelligent, self-assured, and can wear things in a magnificent way. We loved that for Moira.

I love working with actors. I like to listen to how they think about their character. I find this very helpful when it comes to putting the clothes on them, which then becomes their character's skin and expression of who they are. If you get that wrong, many other things can go wrong as well.

Working with Catherine and Dan was such a collaborative experience. Everybody contributed, everybody had something to say, and everybody knew when a look was right. I always say that Catherine was so brave. She was physically brave, but it's also an emotional thing for an actor to put on clothes. We always knew she would respond well to what we were pulling for her. Sometimes I'd think we'd gone too far with a look and she would say, "No, Debra, I think we could do more!"

DANIEL LEVY: As soon as Catherine showed us the pictures of Daphne Guinness, I knew almost instantly where I wanted to go with that inspiration for our character. Moira is a person who is both completely confident and at the same time so fearful of letting people in. I think it was an integral part of her character that in certain cases her clothes acted as armor, as a form of protection. But they're also a form of self-expression. She is a woman who is not fearful of her age or of being sexy, and that really opened the floodgates for us in terms of the endless options we would have when it came to what Moira would wear.

CATHERINE O'HARA: It's one thing to say, "Oh, I want to have this vibe. I want to be someone who thinks she's young and hip and fearless and wears incredible clothes." You can all agree on any number of ideas, but when it comes down to actually finding the pieces and making them work on the body, I had nothing to do with that. That was all Daniel and Debra Hanson.

From day one, when I saw the pieces that Daniel and Deb had pulled for me, I thought, "Oh my god, this is even way more exciting than what I was thinking." And every single wardrobe fitting was a thrill.

MOIRACABULARY

CATHERINE O'HARA: I love arcane vocabulary words and I felt that Moira would, too. It's just another example of her believing that she has so much wisdom to impart to those around her. In the first season of our show, our makeup artist, Lucky Bromhead, gave me a copy of the book *Foyle's Philavery: A Treasury of Unusual Words*. I became very attached to it and I began to replace some of the words in my scripts with new words I'd found in the book.

FAN ART BY GREG ROBERTSON

ABHORRENT: causing strong dislike or hatred

ACCOLADES: expressions of praise

ACQUIESCE: to accept, comply, or submit

ADULATION: flattery; excessive admiration

AILUROPHOBE: a person who hates or fears cats

ALLEGORY: a symbolic representation, often in literature or poetry

ANNULLED: reduced to nothing; made invalid

ASSAILED: attacked or confronted violently or energetically

ASSUAGE: to lessen the intensity of something that pains or distresses

BAILIWICK: the area in which one has superior knowledge or authority

BALATRON: a buffoon; one who speaks nonsense

BÉBÉ: baby

BEDAZZLE: to enchant; also to cover with jewels or other decorations

BEDEVILED: caused distress or trouble

BENEFICENCE: the act or quality of doing or producing good

BESTIAL: beast-like

BICORN: two-horned, also crescent-like

BLIGHTED: impaired, rotted, or destroyed

BLOUSON: blousing garment

BOLUS: a rounded mass, such as a large pill

BOMBILATING: buzzing or droning with sound

BRAMBLY: prickly

BUCOLIC: relating to shepherds or typical rural life

CALLIPYGIAN: having shapely buttocks

CANOODLING: engaging in amorous embracing, caressing, and kissing

CANTICLE: song

CAPRICIOUS: impulsive, unpredictable

CHANTEUSE: a female singer

CHIN-WAG: a friendly conversation

CHOCKABLOCK: full, crowded

CHURLISH: lacking civility or graciousness

CLANGOROUS: marked by loud banging

CLOTHIER: a person who makes or sells clothing

CLOYING: excessively sweet or sentimental

COGITATION: the act of pondering or thinking intently about something

COGNOSCENTI: a person with expert knowledge in a subject

COIFFURE: hairstyle; manner of arranging hair

COLOSSAL: of great bulk, extent, or power

COMMEDIA DEL COMMODE: bathroom humor (loosely translated)

CONFAB: a discussion or conference

CONFABULATE: to talk informally or hold a discussion

CORNUCOPIA: an inexhaustible store or abundance

CORTEGE: a following of attendants

CORVIDAE: a family of birds including ravens, crows, magpies, or jays

COUP D'ETAT: the violent overthrow of leadership by a small group

CRESTFALLEN: feeling shame or humiliation

DALLIANCE: a casual romantic relationship

DANGERSOME: dangerous

DEBAUCHERY: indulgence in behavior involving sex, drugs, alcohol, etc. and/or considered immoral

DÉCLASSÉ: of lower class or inferior status

DELUGE: a drenching rain or an overwhelming amount of something

DEPRECATORY: apologetic

DEWDROPPER: a lazy young man

DIRIGIBLE: an airship

DISCIPLES: followers

DISCOMFITURE: in a state of embarrassment or having frustrated plans

DISCONSOLATE: downcast or cheerless

DISGRUNTLED: annoyed or unhappy

DODDY-POLE: a fool or silly person

DRAGOONED: forced into submission or compliance

DUPLICITOUS: two-faced or deceptive

EBRIOUS: drunk or tipsy

EFFERVESCENCE: a lively or bubbly quality

EFFUSIVE: expressing feelings of gratitude or pleasure

ELEPHANTINE: clumsy or ponderous

ENCUMBERED: burdened or weighed down

ENNUI: boredom

ENSCONCE: to settle oneself in a safe, comfortable, or secret place

ENURESIS: involuntary discharge of urine

ENVISAGE: to have a mental picture of, especially in advance of realization

EPISTLE: a letter

FETED: celebrated with an elaborate party

FOREBODING: a feeling that something bad will happen

FRANGIBLE: fragile or easily broken

FRIPPET: a frivolous young woman

FULSOME: characterized by abundance or generous in amount

GAWPUS: a lazy person

GESTATED: conceived of and gradually developed a thought in the mind

GLEE-RIDDEN: dominated or overcome by delight

GOBSMACKED: overwhelmed with surprise or shock

GRINAGOG: a foolish, grinning person

GROTTO: a cave

HABILIMENTED: clothed

HEURISTIC: relating to exploratory problem-solving technique or trial and error

ILLUSTRIOUS: notably outstanding due to achievements or actions

IMAGINATORS: people who imagine or create

IMPROMPTU: spur of the moment, without previous preparation

INAMORATA: a woman with whom one has romantic or intimate relations

INGENUE: a naïve girl or young woman

IRKSOME: annoying or irritating

JABBERWOCKY: meaningless words

JAPE: a practical joke

JUVENESCENCE: the state of being youthful

KATZENJAMMER: distress or discordant clamor

KISMETIC: characterized by fate

LADEN: carrying a load or burden

LARGESSE: generous giving of gifts or money to others

LINCHPIN: key element that serves to hold together parts that exist or function as a unit

LOTHARIO: a man who seduces women

LUNETTES: glasses (Fr.)

LUPANARIAN: brothel-like

MAMMAE: mammary glands; breasts

MANHANDLED: handled roughly

MELODRAMATIC: an over-the-top appeal to emotions

MERCANTILE: relating to trade or commerce

MERCURIAL: characterized by unpredictable or changeable mood

MISE-EN-SCÈNE: the arrangement of actors and scenery on a stage for a theatrical production

MISSIVE: a written communication

MONOLITH: a massive structure

NEPOTISM: favoritism based on a family relationship

NUDNIK: an annoying person or jerk

NUGATORY: of little or no consequence

OBSIDIAN: deep black, like the dark natural glass formed by the cooling of molten lava

ODIOUS: arousing hatred

OENOLOGICAL: the science and study of wine and wine making

OVERZEALOUSNESS: showing too much eagerness

OVUM: an egg

OXIDIZE: to rust or dry up

PABLUM: a bland or overly simplistic sentiment

PALPATE: examine by touch

PARLEY: to speak with another

PATRICIAN: belonging to the aristocracy

PAWKY: artfully shrewd

PECCADILLOES: slight offenses

PECKISH: hungry

PECUNIARY: relating to money

PENCHANT: a strong inclination or liking

PENURY: extreme frugality

PEREGRINATION: travel, especially on foot

PERQUISITE: gratuity or tip; profit incidental to regular salary or wages

PETTIFOGGING: quibbling over trifles

PILFER: to steal stealthily in small amounts

PIQUE: (a fit of) a feeling of wounded vanity or resentment

PLACATION: to soothe by making concessions

PODUNK: a small, unimportant, and isolated town

POTABLE: suitable for drinking

PRECURSOR: a thing or event that precedes another

PREDILECTION: a preference or special liking for something

PRESTIDIGITATOR: a person who performs a sleight of hand; someone nimble and quick

PROFICIENCIES: advanced knowledge or skills

PROLETARIAN: a member of the laboring class

PROPITIOUS: being of a favorable sign or good omen

QUAGMIRE: a difficult or entrapping situation

QUANDARY: a state of confusion or doubt

REBUFFING: rejecting or snubbing

RECIPROCITY: a mutual exchange of favors or privileges

REDOLENCE: evocative scent or aroma

RENEGADE: a person who rejects lawful or conventional behavior

REPAST: a meal

REPOSE: a state of rest after exertion

REPUTE: the state of being favorably known, spoken of, or esteemed

RETICENCE: the quality or state of being reserved or restrained

REYNARD: a fox

SAGACITY: discernment or far-sightedness

SALACIOUS: arousing or appealing to sexual desire or imagination

SCINTILLA: a trace or spark of something

SCORDATURA: the technique of altering the tuning of a stringed instrument to achieve a particular effect

SCRUM: a usually tightly packed or disorderly crowd

SELF-EFFACEMENT: the state of keeping oneself in an inconspicuous role or position especially due to modesty or shyness

SELF-FLAGELLATE: extreme criticism of oneself

SERENDIPITOUS: the faculty or phenomenon of finding valuable or agreeable things not sought for

SINGULTUS: hiccup

SKULLDUGGERY: underhanded or unscrupulous behavior; also a devious action or trick

SOIREE: a party or reception held in the evening

SPANANDRY: the scarcity of a male population

SQUIRE: to escort

SUBTERFUGE: a deceptive action or strategy

SUFFONSIFYING: satisfying

SUP: to eat the evening meal

TANNENBAUM: a fir tree

TESTUDINE: a turtle

TÊTE-À-TÊTE: a private conversation between two people

THAUMATURGY: the performance of miracles or magic

THESPIAN: actor

THRONGS: large, densely packed crowds of people or animals

TIMOROUS: the state or quality of being timid or fearful

TITILLATING: pleasantly stimulating or exciting; also erotic

TITULAR: bearing the title; titled

TOGGERY: clothing

UNASINOUS: sharing or displaying in unison stupidity or foolishness

VERITABLY: being in fact the thing named and not false, unreal, or imaginary

VESTMENTS: clothing

VISAGE: the face or appearance of a person or sometimes an animal

VIVACITY: lively in temper or spirit

VOCIFEROUS: loud or insistent

WAGGISH: the state of being mischievous or humorous

WAYFARING: characterized by traveling, especially on foot

WHIMSICAL: lightly fanciful

WINSOME: cheerful or lighthearted

Behind the Episode

Fold in the cheese.

CATHERINE O'HARA: I believe the "fold in the cheese" scene was one of the first scenes Daniel and I did alone. I thought it was funny on paper and it was really fun to shoot. But, because Daniel and I both played the frustration and awkwardness of David and Moira trying to cook together for the first time and failing miserably, I was surprised to hear from several people the next week that the edit of the scene was hilarious. I have to agree. Neither David nor Moira can admit they're in way over their heads. Stupid and cocky, in comedy you can't lose with that combination.

DANIEL LEVY: I always loved when David and Moira tried to do something together—my mind goes to their "Allez-Vous" scheme and all the other schemes that they concocted together. In those early days, whether they admitted it or not, they definitely enjoyed each other's company.

Personally, I think Moira is one of the coolest women I have ever met. From David's perspective, regardless of the mothering that did or didn't happen, I think he always admired Moira and aspired to be like her. Moira has great taste, she's incredibly self-assured, she knows what she wants. I think for David, specifically, that's a big deal because he so often feels like he doesn't know what he wants at all. To combat that feeling he tries to be like Moira in superficial ways. He'll dress like Moira and act like Moira, but what was missing in their relationship was real closeness. What they're learning now is how to be a family instead of just two people that have coexisted.

And then, of course, getting to play the straight man to Catherine in this scene was such a joy, and also such an incredible challenge, because I'm notoriously not good at keeping a straight face. I probably broke more than anybody on the show, so I really had to take that moment very seriously and not laugh when Catherine started to scream and ad-libbed the line "What does burning smell like?!"

BEHIND THE SCENES
Dan and Catherine on set for episode 202 "Family Dinner."
April 21, 2015

FAN ART BY JO BEN-SHMUEL

She picks up the recipe and reads:

>   MOIRA (CONT'D)
> Now try to keep up. The next step
> is to fold in the cheese.

David looks at her.

>   DAVID
> What does that mean? What does
> "fold in cheese" mean?

Moira clearly doesn't know.

>   MOIRA
> You just fold it.

>   DAVID
>   (trying to remain calm)
> I understand that, but how do you
> fold it? Do you fold it like a
> piece of paper then drop it in?

>   MOIRA
> Do I have to show you everything?

>   DAVID
> Well, you can show me one thing.

>   MOIRA
> It says to fold it!

>   DAVID
> We've established what it says!

>   MOIRA
> I don't know how to be clearer! You
> take the cheese and you --

>   DAVID
> If you say "fold it" one more
> time...

>   MOIRA
> It says to fold it!

>   DAVID
> You're the one who made these. You
> fold it.

He walks into the dining room. She turns back to the stove.

>   MOIRA
> David? The sauce is bubbling all
> up.... It smells like burning...
> David.

BEHIND THE SCENES
Original script from "Family Dinner."

Behind the Episode

Moira's audition.

CATHERINE O'HARA: I think Moira is the most threatened of all the family by this small-town life because she actually came from a small town and got out. So she tries to resist it, but at the same time she knows she can easily get sucked back into it because it's the life she knew.

But when she heard that the women in the town had a singing group, she thought it was absurd of them not to ask her, an experienced professional, to join them, if only to teach them a thing or two. But, the truth is, she loves any chance to sing and show off her many talents. And when she learned that Jocelyn might actually take the open position on the Town Council, it was a kind of survival instinct in Moira that kicked in. She knew that council decisions could affect her family's chances of getting out of town, and I think that's what made her announce a run for office. But she had no idea how wonderfully rewarding both the Jazzagals and Town Council experiences would turn out to be.

I love that Moira was able to get out of the motel room in season two and have some new adventures with the Jazzagals and with the Town Council. All those scenes were fun for me to play and I loved working with all those lovely actors and friends.

Performances

LITTLE TOWNS, BIG VOICES FESTIVAL
CENTRAL PARK, NEW YORK

SCHITT'S CREEK TOWN HALL CONCERT

SCHITT'S CREEK HIGH SCHOOL GRADUATION CEREMONY

ROSE FAMILY CHRISTMAS PARTY

YARN-FOR-CHEAP CONCERT

THE MARRIAGE OF PATRICK BREWER AND DAVID ROSE

Set List

IT'S RAINING MEN 203

ISLANDS IN THE STREAM 305

BABY, I'M YOURS 313

TAKIN' IT HOME 408

SILENT NIGHT 413

NINE INCH NAILS MEDLEY 503
FEATURING
"I WANT TO KISS YOU LIKE AN ANIMAL"

POISON MEDLEY 506

PRECIOUS LOVE 614

THE BEST 614

FAN ART BY KORY MCGEEHAN
COMPILED BY @SCHITTSSHEETS

In conversation with

SARAH LEVY, KAREN ROBINSON, *and* **JENNIFER ROBERTSON**

On singing with the Jazzagals.

SL The Jazzagals! The Jazzagals was one of my absolute favorite parts about working on *Schitt's Creek*. I wouldn't call myself a singer in any professional sense, but I can and love to sing, so this was a dream come true. We spent hours in rehearsal on these songs, masterfully arranged by Aaron Jensen, which truly made it feel as though we were a real a cappella group. It was also such an exciting moment when we could finally take what we had been working on to set and let everyone hear it for the first time. I think we all had a great sense of pride in what we had accomplished.

Being a part of the Jazzagals was not only special because of the material we were working on, but also that we got to do it with such a kind, talented group of women. What I loved about this group was that we were all incredibly supportive of each other both on and off screen. It became a very safe space to be vulnerable and laugh and cry, as well as sing, and that was not something I anticipated as we began the Jazzagals journey. To that point, it didn't surprise me one bit that Twyla would be a part of this group. If the café didn't feed her soul quite enough, I think the Jazzagals topped it off.

KR The introduction of the Jazzagals was such an unexpected pleasure. They were really a stroke of genius, because they served as an additional platform to showcase the immense talent of the cast members and allowed insight into their characters' lives and relationships with each other in detailed and understated ways.

JR Most of the Jazzagals are unbelievable singers. Like award-winning singers! So to be in that group of ladies was so joyful, and they were so supportive of me. I am not a singer, but I can sing when I am guided along, so they always put me next to somebody very strong, like Divine Brown or Lili Connor, so that I could find my harmony. I'd call them my "hearing-ear person." It was so much fun rehearsing with those ladies and then singing in front of the cast when we did a scene.

KR I can hold my own with a harmony, but those women could *sing!* I couldn't believe how much fun I was having working with them. Aaron Jensen's arrangements were divine. They were complex, textured, and unbelievably harmonious. I still sing them to myself.

SL What I dream about is a Jazzagals album in which the world could hear a full-length version of the songs, because they could literally bring you to tears, they were so beautiful and pure. I would sometimes catch my dad with his headphones on, listening to the recorded version of the songs on repeat. He loves a good harmony.

JR Eugene loved every second of it. I remember Dan said, "There was no greater joy than me watching my dad watching other people sing, because he *lives* for it." It was so sweet and so charming.

BEHIND THE SCENES
(BACK ROW, FROM LEFT) Marilyn Bellfontaine, Jacquelyn French, Jennifer Foster, Divine Brown, Christina Song, and Mary Kelly.
(FRONT ROW) Karen, Catherine, Jenn, and Sarah. The Jazzagals all together on set for episode 613 "Start Spreading the News."
May 13, 2019

BEHIND THE SCENES
Annie and Tim on location for episode 204, "Estate Sale."
June 29, 2015

FAN ART BY BUNNY PERNO-HORNE

Behind the Episode

Wendy and the Blouse Barn.

ROBIN DUKE: Playing Wendy was a lot of fun. I've known Dan since he was a baby. I'm his mom's friend, so there was that familiarity. I don't know how many times we had to stop a take because I called him Daniel instead of David!

Wendy always seems to be starting over. She's got that Jackie Gleason thing where she's always trying to find that quick-money scheme. But it's not really a scheme. She's actually engaged with whatever she does. Even when it doesn't work out, she moves on to the next project where she can apply her fashion skills and her eye for style.

I think she learned a lot from David in terms of what's going on in today's world of fashion. She needed that boost, that injection of youth into her life. I think she appreciated his knowledge and his enthusiasm for fashion in this small town. Finally, there was somebody that she could talk with who had the same interest as she did. Maybe not the same taste, but certainly there was a knowledge there that they shared, and she loved that.

Behind the Episode

Alexis and Mutt break up.

ANNIE MURPHY: I remember filming this scene. It was Dan and our director, Jerry Ciccoritti, who were working with us. The direction Tim and I kept getting was "more silence and just really sit in it." For a while I think we were really thrown by a scene with so little dialogue, and we were both like, "Fuck, are we doing this right?!" But I think it ended up being exactly that awkward uncertainty that fed the scene and made it successful. I just watched it again recently with my mother—who re-watches *Schitt's Creek* every other month!—and not to toot our own horns at all, but I realized this scene has the feeling of the last scene in *The Graduate* where the cut was never called and it's just the two actors sitting there in the silence, not knowing if they should stop or keep going, which just added a beautiful energy to the scene. I think that there was a similar uncertainty when Tim and I were doing this scene, and it really paid off.

DANIEL LEVY: This was a tough scene to execute because we have to show Alexis and Mutt breaking up without saying anything at all. It's a challenging scene for the actors and it's a big risk for the writers because you're relying heavily on execution. But obviously, between Tim and Annie, we knew that we had very capable actors.

I remember in the first couple takes of that scene, our director would yell cut and I would run over and say, "No, no no no. Go back. Let them sit there. Keep that going." Eventually we just let the cameras roll and let Annie and Tim do what they did, and it was quite incredible. To force the audience to be in that moment and sit with the characters in their awkwardness and discomfort, that was the experience that I really wanted. It was one of those early moments in our show that really struck a chord with people.

In conversation with

DUSTIN MILLIGAN *and*
ANNIE MURPHY

On the love that still lingers.

AM　I love Ted and Alexis. As much as people have their soft spot for Mutt, I feel like it was with Ted that Alexis truly learned what love was.

DM　When Ted went away to the couples' retreat alone, he was able to find himself in a way. He returned a new man—a scruffier new man who has a motorcycle and more of a backbone. That created a new dynamic between him and Alexis and shifted the balance of power a bit so he was no longer such a pushover.

AM　Alexis realized the repercussions and impact you can feel when you hurt somebody you love. That's such a formative life experience that she hadn't had until she was 28 or 29 years old. After you feel those things, you are a changed person.

DM　But Ted does still support Alexis despite what happened between them romantically. There's something still lingering there. You can't just turn off all your feelings for someone, and I think for Ted that translated into him just trying to help her expand her perspective beyond what it had been when she first arrived in Schitt's Creek.

AM　Ted really was integral to her growth and a large part of who she became by the end of the series.

In conversation with

EUGENE LEVY *and* **CATHERINE O'HARA**

On the Roses reaching a turning point.

EL   This scene was a turning point for Johnny and for the show. It was a beautifully written scene and one of the more poignant scenes to shoot. The Roses come face-to-face with their former life when they encounter their old friends in the restaurant. There is an expectation that this will drive them deeper into despair when they come to the realization that things will never be as they were. And that's exactly what happens, until Roland and Jocelyn show up. We feel for Roland and Jocelyn in this moment because they are so obviously shunned by the Roses. But, after Johnny and Moira's initial embarrassment, the world takes on a different hue for Johnny as he listens to his former friends bad-mouthing the wine, the hors d'oeuvres, the restaurant, and finally the town. Johnny finds himself defending Schitt's Creek and his new friends, Roland and Jocelyn. This turn of events turns out to nail the lid shut on their old life.

CO   This scene just killed me. I cried every single time Eugene gave that speech. He is such a good actor and Johnny was so sincere and open in that moment. It was as if he (Johnny) was caught by surprise by his own feelings—that he actually was grateful for the town's open arms that took in his family at their worst moment. He was so broken, in a good life-changing way, that there was a wonderful release in stating his gratitude out loud. And as Moira, it killed me to see my husband broken. I didn't want to hear what he was saying, but I couldn't deny it was true, and it made me love Johnny all the more.

EL   This was a big change for Johnny. And Moira, to some extent, as she was always the last Rose to want to settle for a future in this town. And it was a turning point in the show. For the remainder of our six seasons, the Roses continue to settle more comfortably into their life in this little town and accept more readily the Schitts and all the townsfolk into their new social circle. They became citizens of Schitt's Creek.

CO   And, by the time we got to Mutt's barn, Johnny and Moira were full of love for each other and their children. Even Moira was able to let go and enjoy the moment— for at least a moment.

Behind the Episode

213 **HAPPY ANNIVERSARY**

The Roses say "I love you."

ANNIE MURPHY: One of my favorite moments from the whole show was the finale from season two when we're all dancing together in the barn. Getting to dance next to Eugene Levy, who's raising the roof for hours on end, was one of the best moments of my life.

CATHERINE O'HARA: It was great fun, all of us dancing together. Dancing is a wonderful creative release and I think we were all basking in each other's sweetness and funny dance moves.

DANIEL LEVY: We had been building toward this scene for two full seasons. There was a lot of emotional foundation to lay before we got to this moment when the Roses say "I love you" for the first time. I remember having a very clear idea of how I wanted the barn to feel. I wanted it to feel warm and special, because this was a moment when the Roses, as well as the audience, look at their surroundings and think, "Oh, this could be okay." The joy and the dancing in that scene was also very real for everybody. Or, at least it was for me!

EUGENE LEVY: The final scene of season two, which saw the Roses dancing as a family in Mutt's barn, was the most joyous scene we experienced in our six years on the show. The Roses, now divorced from their former life, say "I love you" to each other for the first time. Daniel's choice of "Precious Love" as the song we all dance to was perfect. Beyond the highs that the characters were experiencing, we as a cast were also experiencing the love we were truly feeling for each other. After two seasons of watching this brilliant cast of actors give such dimension to their characters and getting to know them as the talented and good-hearted people they are, the emotion underpinning this scene was palpable.

BEHIND THE SCENES
The cast on set for the finale of season two, dancing in celebration to James Morrison's "Precious Love."
May 22, 2015

"I would be pleased to RSVP as . . . pending."

MOIRA ROSE

season

3

FAN ART BY
JESSICA CRUICKSHANK

SEASON THREE

304

Driving Test

Written by
Michael Short

Directed by
Paul Fox

Alexis drives a stressed-out David to his driving test, and finds herself in the unusual position of coaching her older brother. As the new owner of the motel, Stevie is in over her head, and Johnny and Moira employ different strategies to discourage her from selling.

301

Opening Night

Written by
Daniel Levy

Directed by
TW Peacocke

David and Stevie are shocked to learn that their romantic lives are intersecting in an unexpected way, while Alexis intersects with Mutt's new romantic interest. Johnny struggles to get a new business venture off the ground, and Moira makes a splash at her first Town Council meeting, but quickly encounters roadblocks from her colleagues.

305

Rooms by the Hour

Written by
Monica Heisey
and Daniel Levy

Directed by
TW Peacocke

Johnny puts the motel in an awkward position after renting rooms to a morally dubious enterprise, while David helps Moira tape a film audition. Alexis convinces Ted that a livestream bunny cam will help advertise the vet clinic. But the camera ends up advertising more than expected.

302

The Throuple

Written by
David West Read

Directed by
TW Peacocke

Johnny offers to help out an injured Twyla by waiting tables at the café, but soon gets in over his head. Alexis and Moira make a plan to have lunch despite their mutual anxiety about spending time alone together. David and Stevie try to figure out the boundaries of their three-way relationship with Jake.

306

Murder Mystery

Written by
Michael Short

Directed by
TW Peacocke

Johnny and Stevie visit a nearby golf course to pitch a package deal with the motel, but Johnny becomes distracted by his desire to play a round of golf. After agreeing to attend Twyla's murder mystery party, Moira must help her recruit other guests. Alexis entertains a suggestion from Ted to go back to school.

303

New Car

Written by
Kevin White

Directed by
Paul Fox

Johnny and Moira feign poverty (and an accent) in an attempt to get a deal on a used car, while David helps Stevie lay her great-aunt to rest. Alexis and Ted negotiate the rules of their professional relationship.

307

General Store

Written by
Daniel Levy

Directed by
Paul Fox

David contemplates starting a new business in town, and Moira uses her seat on Town Council to protect her son's interests. Alexis discovers high school isn't as easy as it used to be. Johnny reluctantly offers romantic advice to Ivan, the hapless baker, in return for help with the motel's continental breakfast.

308

Motel Review

Written by
Kevin White

Directed by
Paul Fox

David meets Ray's new assistant, Patrick, who tries to help him set up his business. Johnny defends Alexis's schoolwork. Moira's hospitality skills are put to the test when she's forced to deal with a high-maintenance motel guest.

309

The Affair

Written by
David West Read

Directed by
TW Peacocke

Moira and Roland find themselves in a compromising situation with their spouses after a night at a regional Town Councilors' conference. As David and Patrick prepare the store for opening, David acts jealous of Alexis's flirting with Patrick.

310

Sebastien Raine

Written by
Kevin White

Directed by
TW Peacocke

David's ex-boyfriend arrives in town to do a photo series on Moira, but Moira soon realizes his intentions might be less than complimentary. Johnny and Roland attend Bob's poker night and attempt to turn the tables on Bob and Gwen. Alexis accompanies Ted to a seniors' dance and begins to reevaluate her relationship with him.

311

Stop Saying Lice!

Written by
Daniel Levy

Directed by
Paul Fox

Moira is wary after Town Council decides to name a questionable flower garden after her—that is, until she learns the real reason behind the dubious honor. Meanwhile, Johnny must do damage control after Alexis brings lice to the motel. In an effort to flee the lice epidemic, David schemes his way into spending the night at Stevie's apartment.

312

Friends & Family

Written by
David West Read

Directed by
Paul Fox

Moira tracks down the Roses' gigantic family portrait as a gift for Johnny, but the family struggles to find a place for it. David organizes a "soft launch" for the new store, but becomes concerned after word begins to spread and the guest list gets out of hand. Alexis and Ted become awkward around each other after sharing a kiss.

313

Grad Night

Written by
Kevin White and
Daniel Levy

Directed by
TW Peacocke

Johnny and Stevie are delighted to have an excuse to put on the motel's "No Vacancy" sign for the first time. While Moira and the Jazzagals prepare for an upcoming festival gig, Alexis gets ready for her high-school graduation and makes a big decision about her future. David is secretly bitter that the family forgot his birthday, but gets closer to Patrick after the two go on an accidental date.

FAN ART BY CARLA MASKALL

Behind the Episode

"What the flying fuck is going on here?"

DANIEL LEVY: Our goal going into the writers' room every season was to try and one-up the season before. In the first few episodes of season three, David and Stevie again find themselves in a romantic entanglement—one that I think is slightly pushing the boundaries in terms of sexuality and comedy. What I like about this dynamic is that it shows how Stevie and David are kind of like the same person, raised in two different environments. What draws them to each other almost instantly is the recognition that there's something in you that is in me that other people don't get.

EMILY HAMPSHIRE: I believe the dynamic between Stevie, David, and Jake may have been stolen from my actual life. As the writing on the show evolved, we started to see some of our *real* lives pop up in scripts. For instance, Alexis wearing natural deodorant or Mr. Rose catching Stevie sexting with Emir. That situation didn't *not* happen to me one time when I was trying to show Eugene a cute pic I took of Dan's dog Redmond on my phone and accidentally scrolled a *little* too far.

Alexis: "What is your favorite season?"

Moira: "Awards."

DANIEL LEVY: Who could predict that this moment between Alexis and Moira from episode 302, "The Throuple," would turn into the most shared meme of our entire show?

In conversation with

CATHERINE O'HARA
and **ANNIE MURPHY**

On the mother-daughter dynamic.

AM   I treasured any scene I was in with just Catherine, because it's *Catherine O'Hara*. It never got old. I think the lunch scene in the café really shows that Alexis longed for Moira to be more of a mother figure and it just took some time for Moira to figure out for herself what that meant.

CO   I like to think Moira and her mother were not that close and she never had a good example of how to be really close to a daughter. As much as Moira wants to be close to Alexis, she doesn't quite know how.

AM   I think Moira and Alexis had a bit of a rockier start when they came to Schitt's Creek, whereas Alexis and Johnny are more like two peas in a pod. Still, Alexis looks up to Moira, and I think that there are great similarities between them that neither of them wishes to acknowledge. It's nice that they start to make a concerted effort to try and build their relationship, as difficult as it might be.

CO   Fortunately, Alexis keeps offering Moira opportunities to become the mother she assumed she already was.

AM   In each scene between the two of them they kind of chip away toward their own version of a mother-daughter relationship and end up in a genuinely loving place.

CO   How can one not fall in love with Alexis?!

Behind the Episode

303 **NEW CAR**

The vintage Lincoln.

DANIEL LEVY: There were a lot of conversations about the car that were similar to conversations we had about the aesthetic of the motel. We still wanted the car to feel special even though it wasn't new or a status vehicle. We wanted it to still have a level of pride.

What I love about this car is that, back in its day, it was actually a showy car. Sure, it's lost its status and luster, but it has a level of respectability to it just in the sheer size of it. We thought it would be a great mirroring of our family. It's all they could afford and yet they still managed to find a car that didn't say "we give up." There's a sense of pride and celebration to it when Johnny and Moira bring it back to the motel.

It also lent itself to some great comedic moments. It was like driving a boat, and those doors weighed about a hundred pounds each, so when you get a prop like that to play with, it only helps you as an actor.

I don't know who has that car now. It really was a keeper, and I wish I had kept it.

Behind the Episode

304 DRIVING TEST

David, nobody cares.

DANIEL LEVY: We really tried to be extra thoughtful when we wrote important scenes that were meant to be moments that would bring our characters closer together. I think the biggest challenge as a writer is that you never want the show to feel heavy-handed or saccharine. You want it to be funny but also have moments of sentimentality that feel earned and not cheap or tinny.

The driving test felt like the perfect backdrop for David and Alexis to have a revelatory discussion about their past. It starts off as a petty fight, but it's ultimately revealed to be rooted in David's resentment that he had to take care of his sister for most of his life because their parents never did. Johnny and Moira were too preoccupied with their own stuff to really care for their kids emotionally.

In the writers' room we discussed the concept that arguments within a family are always rooted in something much deeper than what they initially start out as, and that was a theme for us as we continued to peel back the layers on these characters.

I think David really struggled to find his identity because he was lacking love in his life. I used a lot of my own revelations to create Alexis's dialogue and the tension in this scene. The concept that "nobody cares" was a big awakening for me in my early twenties. The idea that nobody's thinking about you the way you're thinking about you was a concept that really set me free, and I think it was a valuable lesson for David as well.

Again, I'm just so grateful for our cast and that we had the right people in the right place at the right time, because that moment in the later scene when Alexis looks out the window and smiles could have really gone south if it weren't in such capable hands. Annie is the queen of those hidden moments. She makes them feel real and profound in a way that doesn't tip the scales or violate the boundaries of the comedic world of our show.

ALEXIS	So I assume you got your license and you're not just driving us home illegally.	**ALEXIS**	See? I told you. He didn't care. You never trust me.
DAVID	I did.	**DAVID**	Yes I do.
ALEXIS	Good.	**ALEXIS**	No you don't.
DAVID	I know.	**DAVID**	Yes I do.
ALEXIS	How was your tester guy? Was he a monster?	**ALEXIS**	No, and you never take my advice, and I'm always the last person you turn to.
DAVID	He was fine.		

DAVID Okay. You want to talk trust? Stevie and Mom weren't running around the world for a decade and a half with random men leaving me at home to wonder whether they were okay.

ALEXIS Well, I'm sorry for having fun, David. With a selection of very confident international men. But I was always okay.

DAVID Were you? Because I was the one at the consulate sending you temporary passports and colored contact lenses whenever you needed them. I was the one at home not having fun because I was constantly worried which East Asian palace Alexis was being held hostage in this week. Not Mom and Dad. Me.

ALEXIS Well, you didn't have to worry about me!

DAVID Well, I did.

In conversation with

DANIEL LEVY *and*
ANNIE MURPHY

On the brother-sister relationship

AM   I don't have any siblings myself, but right out of the gate, Dan and I had a very intense sibling energy between us. I always say that I feel like Dan and I were in this life together, like we had known each other before. Playing that dynamic between David and Alexis was so much fun because we got to act like petulant little kids for the majority of the early seasons. I think David and Alexis acted this way with each other because they'd been apart so much growing up. With Alexis flitting off on her world travels and leaving David mostly at home alone, they hadn't really had those pre-pubescent fights and so they were making up for it by going through that in their late twenties and early thirties.

DL   I think in those early seasons we really wanted to play up the fact that these two didn't have a conventional childhood. They never existed in close proximity, so whereas most siblings would bond and fight over the inescapable reality that they're going to be tied to each other for at least eighteen years, that wasn't the case for those two. My dad and I loved the idea that there would be this instant regression where they would slide into these childish dynamics because they'd never experienced them before. And, of course, that was so fun to play with Annie, because from day one our general dynamic has been very "brother and sister."

AM   I think the "you get murdered first" scene really painted a very clear picture of where they were as people and as siblings.

DL   And the bike riding scene. The thing that I loved about that scene was it involved the whole family. It was the first time that the family was seeing a member of their team succeed at something, even if it's something like their grown son learning to ride a bike! We never wanted to be too heavy-handed in those moments, so it had to be something that was oddly humiliating. The reality of the situation was inherently funny, but there was something underneath it that felt quite warm and supportive.

AM   The other scene that stands out to me was later in season two when Alexis has broken up with Mutt and asks David for a hug. It's such a genuine need on her part for some kind of brotherly love. I think that moment really demonstrated the fact that despite their tumultuous upbringing, they love each other so deeply and they truly are each other's best friends and they have been forever.

DL   Moments like that were really integral to the growth of their relationship because everything for them was new. David kind of looks around as if someone else was in the room and realizes that, oh no, his sister was asking him for a hug and he really doesn't quite know what to do with it. Those were the great scenes to get to write, because it took a while to earn them. We had to lay a lot of track and have David and Alexis at each other's throats in order to land those rare moments when they really needed each other and showed up for each other in unexpected ways.

BEHIND THE SCENES
Dan and Annie.

FAN ART BY BRANDON LORD

154

FAN ART BY STEVE SIZER

"LOVE THAT JOURNEY FOR me"
THE ADVENTURES OF Alexis Rose

1. "There was that time [Stavros] never met me in Rio."

2. "Um, I drove into the Prada store on Rodeo Drive. In fairness, it did look a lot like, um, the entrance to a parking garage . . . And I was high at the time."

3. "One time I escaped from a Thai drug lord's car trunk by bribing him with sex."

4. "Dubai, 2010. I had to pick you up from that blind date that went terribly wrong."

5. "I went on a blind date to Bali with Leo, so I'm pretty sure I'm gonna be fine."

6. "Honestly, Twy, ixnay on the ongsay. Because I tried it once and the guy ripped the guitar out of my hands and he just started smashing it on the ground. Granted, I'm tone deaf and he was a super angry marine, but . . ."

7. "The actual longest relationship was a three-month affair with a Saudi prince, but for the last two months of that I was trapped in his palace trying to get to an embassy."

8. "Do I have to remind you of that time I was taken hostage on David G.'s yacht . . . ?"

9. *"Oh, what, there was no gap year in Belgium? No Tour de France boyfriend?* Yeah, but I never had to ride the bike."

10. "Like, have you ever had to negotiate in Arabic? It is very difficult."

11. "Try getting in to Kiss Kiss in Tokyo without a lock of human hair."

12. "I had a friend in Venice Beach who sold raw milk and his entire compound was raided. I mean, he also sold drugs, but like . . ."

13. "It's just a checkpoint, okay? I've been through tons of these in Johannesburg. It's like a drive-thru, except everybody has a gun."

14. "I've dated enough Wall Street losers to know that 'making things liquid' is not a good thing."

15. "I once dated this sultan's nephew who was forbidden to talk to me or even to look at me, and we made it work for, like, half a regime change, so . . ."

16. "Um, I'm sorry. Were you picked up by the South Korean Secret Police on New Year's?"

17. "So on a scale of one to a São Paolo hangover how are we feeling right now?"

18. *"Bordeaux? The trip I planned for the two of us?* That was a wine tasting tour and I was seven years old."

19 "I have my license in seven different countries, and I have my F class . . . I had a lot of people to move."

20 "You try parallel parking in a burka, David. No amount of flirting can get you out of that. Trust me."

21 "I once had a seven-year-old drive me around Mumbai."

22 "I was constantly worried which East Asian palace Alexis was being held hostage in this week."

23 "I should never have taken that semester off. But I did meet Beyoncé in Mykonos, so it was almost worth it."

24 "Alexis, we sent you to high school in Switzerland because we trusted you."

25 "It reminds me when I was in Bangkok. There was this amazing little resto-lounge that specialized in Tahitian food and scalp massages."

26 "It's the exact same move that I used with my klepto friends in the Hamptons."

27 "Mmm, you learn pretty quickly when you're in a Ugandan diamond smuggler's villa playing for your friend's freedom."

28 "I basically did exactly the same thing with my friends once, but instead of cookies it was whatever we could find in our parents' medicine cabinets and instead of a Christmas party, it was an old boot factory in Krakow."

29 "Alexis and Stavros are on his father's yacht by now, off to Capri."

30 "Tell that to me at 21, escaping the Yakuza."

31 "You took me to the Playboy mansion when I was seven."

32 "Okay, I've just been to Miami so many times before, and trust me, the 'wildlife' is not as sexy up close."

33 "Or the placement of Alexis's back tattoo . . . It says 'that's hot' in Cantonese. Got it in Hong Kong."

34 "Turkish *Cosmo* once included my photo on their list of the world's best sarongs. So let's just say I know my way around a beach."

35 "I fit my high-school best friend in a suitcase way smaller than this when we were crossing the border between Laos and Vietnam, so I'm pretty sure I can figure this out."

36 "I once planned Megan F.'s bachelorette on this tiny island off the coast of Montenegro where nothing is illegal. Like nothing."

37 "I did that with Harry S. and England was, like, too rainy."

38 "So, thank you, my weekend with Tom H. . . . England is here."

FAN ART BY JILLIAN GOELER
COMPILED BY @SCHITTSSHEETS

Behind the Episode

306 **MURDER MYSTERY**

"Chris never tired of trying to get me to laugh."

EUGENE LEVY: I was so excited to be working with Chris Elliott. I've always been such a big fan. Watching him on the old *Late Show with David Letterman* was always a highlight. I can't really put my finger on exactly why he, as a writer, made me laugh so hard. His sense of comedy was definitely located in what I would call a netherworld of conceptual abstraction. But it was his commitment as a performer to pull off this conceit on the Letterman show that really got to my funny bone and I knew that his ne'er-do-well persona that he nurtured over the years was the perfect fit for Roland Schitt.

Chris always reminded me and everyone on set that we were working on a comedy; the idea being that if you're working on a comedy you should be having fun. He always had insanely funny interactions with our crew members, and they loved it every time he was on set. He also had his playful moments with me, in particular, both on and off camera, as he had most of his scenes with me during the series. Chris never tired of trying to get me to laugh right up until the director called "action."

Shooting the golf lesson scene in episode 306 was truly frightening for me because I could not stop laughing. I knew I was in a danger zone standing that close behind Chris because I knew it wouldn't take much for me to lose it. So, when Johnny asks Roland, "And your hands are comfortably gripping the shaft?" and I hear Chris ad-lib, "Oh, they're on the shaft all right," that was all it took. The floodgates opened. No matter how many times we attempted the scene, I couldn't get through it. The director, increasingly upset, came on the set three times, worried that we were losing the afternoon light and might not complete the scene. No pressure! I truly don't know how, but I did get through it. That was always a risk in every scene I had with Chris.

BEHIND THE SCENES
Eugene breaking character while shooting "Murder Mystery"
with Chris on location.

Behind the Episode

Ray Butani: A brand.

RIZWAN MANJI: Something that people may not realize is that all of the brochures, mouse pads, and other promotional items in Ray's office are real pieces created by the design team. I still have some of the travel pamphlets and I have so many of Ray's business cards. I gave a bunch of them as a gift to my kid's teacher, who was a huge fan of *Schitt's Creek*.

The photo of Ray that's everywhere, including on the bench outside Town Hall and at the Christmas tree farm, was actually from a snapshot that was on my iPhone. I remember I was at brunch with a friend and the show called to say, "We need some artwork, can you send us a photo?" Right then and there I asked my friend to take a photo on my phone and I sent it back and said, "Hey, how about this?" It was just a random photo of me from a restaurant in LA and now it's the face of Ray all around Schitt's Creek.

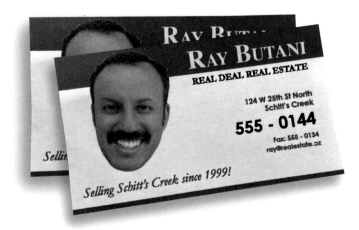

PROP: Ray's business cards from Rizwan's personal collection.

Behind the Episode

David meets Patrick.

NOAH REID: About halfway through season three, Patrick Brewer finds his way into the strange and wonderful world of the Roses. David comes to Ray's office for an application for a business loan. He has an idea for what Patrick thinks could actually be a successful business, but it's completely disorganized and undercooked—David being more of a dreamer than a practical man. From Patrick's perspective, there's a sense of opportunity there, but also a sense of intrigue around a more personal relationship. I'm not sure if in this moment Patrick really recognizes it as a romantic possibility, but there's just something that clicks with him about David. Some kind of common understanding, an easy back-and-forth repartee. As they eventually work toward going into business together, they realize that they can each offer something that the other person can't in order to move a business forward. But then there's also a personal relationship that develops quite naturally over the course of that time and ends with a very potent moment in the season three finale in Patrick's car with their first kiss. It's a pretty huge life moment for Patrick, and for David as well. And, certainly, the beginning of something bigger in the story of *Schitt's Creek*.

DANIEL LEVY: What we wanted to express by introducing Patrick and Rose Apothecary was that David actually had something to offer. I think David had been the butt of many jokes that he himself created or had fallen victim to. So, it would be natural for the audience to at first think, "Oh, another spoiled decision made by David Rose." But then Patrick, upon hearing the concept for this general store, knew that there was actually something smart and thoughtful about what he wanted to do.

The humor then lay in the fact that David was completely incapable of executing. Not that his ideas were bad, not that his taste was off, but just that he was coddled for so long that he had no life skills or enough follow-through to get it off the ground, which made for the perfect entry for Patrick.

It set up Patrick in a way that was so necessary for David. We were establishing him as a really steady, smart, authoritative new voice in David's life. Someone who really didn't care about his frivolity but saw something quite fundamental in him as both a business partner and then eventually a love interest. David never had that before. He's always been the ringleader, the person who's curating gallery events. So the fact that someone comes into his life with such a calm sense of self and such a charming, authoritative presence almost allows David to let his guard down in a professional context and then subliminally he was able to let his guard down in an emotional context as well.

FAN ART BY C. CIMORONI

> DAVID
> I'm here to fill out my
> incorporation papers, for my
> business?

> RAY
> Ah. That's right.
> (to O.S.)
> Patrick!

A young man, PATRICK, approaches from the back.

> RAY (CONT'D)
> Can you please help David here with
> his business paperwork?
> (to couple)
> Okay, you two. Your parents tell me
> you're very sporty. Will, take the
> paddle. And Teresa, let's go
> badminton racket.

Patrick waves David over. He stands to greet David.

> DAVID
> Hi...

> PATRICK
> Patrick.

> DAVID
> I'm--

> PATRICK
> David Rose. You bought the General
> Store.

> DAVID
> Leased. Leased the General Store.

> PATRICK
> That's a big deal.

> DAVID
> Is it?

> PATRICK
> Pretty big. Yeah. Take a seat.

David sits down, encouraged by Patrick's efficiency.

> PATRICK (CONT'D)
> Okay. So. Let's start with the name
> of the company.

(CONTINUED)

> DAVID
> I'm oscillating between two at the
> moment.

> PATRICK
> Okay.

> DAVID
> Can we maybe leave that blank for
> now?

> PATRICK
> Sure. Give you more time to... um,
> oscillate. Business address?

> DAVID
> Okay, I'm in the middle of figuring
> that out. I currently live in a
> motel.
> Which might be confusing since it's
> the address for another business.

> PATRICK
> Okay. So we'll leave that one blank
> too. Batting 1000 here, David.

> DAVID
> I don't know what that means.

Patrick can't help but find this amusing.

> PATRICK
> Here's an easy one: a brief
> description of the business.

> DAVID
> How brief?

> PATRICK
> Just a sentence or two.

> DAVID
> Okay. It's a 'general store' but
> it's also a very specific store.
> But it's not just a store, it's
> also a place to sit and have a
> coffee or a drink but it's not a
> coffee shop or a bar...

BEHIND THE SCENES
Original script for "Motel Review."

FAN ART BY NOELLE SMITH

BUILDING THE APOTHECARY

"It's a general store, but it's also a very specific store."

DAVID ROSE

BRENDAN SMITH: We very much wanted the Rose Apothecary to be a bright, welcoming store. A place where you would look in through the windows and be immediately drawn inside. We also didn't want it to intimidate the townspeople, but instead feel a little familiar to them. Bringing in the older wooden elements, the shelves and big wooden tables, created this familiar feeling, and worked well in contrast to the rather trendy bottles of hand cream and "body milk."

DANIEL LEVY: It was really important that we got the store right. We wanted to make sure that it didn't stand out in a bad way in this small town. We (and David) knew that it had to fit in by embracing a smaller town aesthetic, while at the same time lifting it into David's world. It needed to be different from the aggressive job he did transforming the Blouse Barn. He was more thoughtful here about his surroundings and his customer. He was essentially offering a slightly elevated product to the townspeople and saying you deserve nice things.

Rose Apothecary, BP (*before Patrick*)

Rose Apothecary, AP (*after Patrick*)

Behind the Episode

310 SEBASTIEN RAINE

The "garbage bag" dress.

CATHERINE O'HARA: I love scenes that are almost equally sad and funny, and that is how I felt shooting the photo session scene in the field with François Arnaud, who plays Sebastien Raine. The more Moira tried to come off as wonderful, the more awkward and pathetic she actually looked. And François was very good at playing the seductive photographer and taking advantage of my poor Moira. That fantastic ensemble I'm wearing was chosen, as always, by Debra Hanson and Daniel. It was perfectly gorgeous and ridiculous. I believe they had to watch a video tutorial to figure out how to put on that dress!

DANIEL LEVY: I remember buying the Raf Simons dress that Moira wears for this scene. It was from, I believe, his last collection with Jil Sander, which was one of my favorites. It was an incredibly complicated dress, made basically of PVC, and it took three of us to figure out how to tie Catherine into it. The joy of dressing Moira is that you can take huge risks in terms of the clothes, because Catherine can pull off anything. With that dress in particular, I remember really debating whether or not to buy it, because it was slightly outside of our budget, but I knew that if it worked, it could really work. It became one of Moira's most iconic moments.

THE
MOIRA'S
ROSE'S
GARDEN
4856

FAN ART BY RITA GARZA

172

Behind the Episode

311 **STOP SAYING LICE**

"I don't think that there are enough apostrophes."

EUGENE LEVY: I've always loved the tags that start or finish the show, like the one at the end of "Stop Saying Lice!" in front of the rose garden. They're usually family-oriented, really fun scenes where the four of us are together and you just always get a sense of how the family is changing, evolving, and becoming more of a family. Other scenes are fun in their own way, but the core of the show is these four people learning to be a family and that always hits the old heartstrings for me.

Behind the Episode

Baby, I'm yours.

ANNIE MURPHY: "Grad Night" was such a classic situation for Alexis where she acts like she doesn't need or want Moira's support and says, "I'm fine. Don't worry about it, it's totally fine," even though deep down she really wanted her family there. She wanted to be supported, and she wanted them to show up for her and be proud with her of what she's accomplished. She'd done something very significant, something very important in her life, and very much outside of her comfort zone. But when it was made clear to her that they weren't going to be there, she put up her guard.

Then, of course, Moira showing up with such a grand gesture meant the world to Alexis, because I think Moira means the world to Alexis, although she'd never fully say as much. I will admit, though, in that scene the look on my face is not Alexis, that is full Annie Murphy! To have Catherine O'Hara singing to me/Alexis in a very meaningful way was truly extraordinary. It's something I would never have dreamed would ever happen.

AARON JENSEN, MUSICAL DIRECTOR: "Grad Night" was a special episode for me. It was my first time on set, and the first time the Jazzagals were called upon to bring emotional weight to a scene. I was on stage behind the curtain to lead in the group. For each take, I waited for the director to call "action," gave the group a reassuring smile, counted them in, raced offstage before the curtain opened, and beelined to the back of the gym so I could conduct the rest of the song from the audience. I got my cardio covered that day, that's for sure!

PROP: Framed receipt given to David as a birthday present
from Patrick in episode 313, "Grad Night."

"If there is anything remotely sentimental in here,
he is on a date with you right now."

STEVIE BUDD

In conversation with

NOAH REID *and* DANIEL LEVY

On honoring that *important moment.*

NR   I think the original version of this scene for the finale of season three had Patrick more in the driver's seat. I mean he is literally in the driver's seat, but he was also more figuratively in the driver's seat, making the first move. As we got closer to shooting it, I remember Dan calling me and saying, "I don't know that this moment has ever been easy for anyone," so in order to do justice to the emotional reality of the moment, he reconfigured it so Patrick was much more off-balance.

DL   This scene was originally written with Patrick leaning in to kiss David. It's hard to explain, but the scene just never quite sat right with me and I knew something needed to be changed. I ended up calling my friend Salvatore, who actually played Antonio in season five. He's a very dear friend and I called him up and we talked about our first gay kiss and what that meant. The one thing that came out of that discussion about our first experiences is that there's a tremendous amount of fear right before it happens. I think for so many queer people, to act on that impulse in that moment is more than just a first kiss, it's taking an active step out of the closet.

NR   For Patrick, who is used to being very confident, in control, and in charge, he is now experiencing something that he hasn't faced before. I think those moments are quite intense for anybody—they feel huge, your heart is pounding—but certainly for Patrick in this situation, never having kissed a guy or felt that way about a guy before, it would feel almost impossible.

DL   It's interesting because Patrick had really spent the entire season trying to get David's attention and trying to let him know that he has feelings for him. We had that whole scene where Stevie says if he brings something personal as a birthday gift it means that he has feelings for you. But, after speaking with Salvatore, I thought it would be more authentic if this character had spent so much time sort of waving his arms at David saying, "Look at me, I care about you," and yet right before the big moment of the kiss, he couldn't find the courage to do it.

NR   The rewrite felt much more emotionally dialed in and grounded in reality. Dan and I had worked on the new scene a little bit over the phone the day before, and I remember very well sitting outside the motel in that car. It was a night shoot, and I always love a night shoot—there's something about it that takes you out of your natural rhythm. I remember it was really quiet, like the whole crew knew something special was happening. It felt like a big turning point for these characters. This wasn't a typical "will they/won't they" scene, these were real, breathing, feeling human beings figuring something out together.

DL   The other thing that I loved about that scene is that it turned into a pivotal moment for David where he had to step out of his own world of insecurity and doubt, having had his own failed relationships, and make that active choice to say, "OK, I'm going to do something that goes against the trauma of my own previous relationships where I've felt unloved or taken advantage of, and I'm going to try something here." And the minute that choice was made, the whole scene opened up for me. It ended up being this incredibly necessary moment between the two of them where David and the audience were able to see a level of vulnerability in Patrick that they'd never seen before. And David was also able to step out of his shell a little bit and take a risk for the first time. And ultimately that risk paid off because in kissing Patrick, he set him free.

I think when you're dealing with sexuality of that sensitive nature, you really have to take the time to honor the reality of the situation because you're speaking to people, and their experiences that might be similar or different but equally as vulnerable. So, to really honor that moment for people who had experienced it was really crucial and one that I'm very glad and relieved changed and evolved in the way it did.

NR   It felt very real and connected, and it also felt like a nice way to wrap up that storyline for the season, but with so much more ground to cover later. It felt like a really nice door to open going into season four.

*"You have the opportunity to climb
out of the quicksand that was your past
and stand firmly in the present.
Let us celebrate that."*

MOIRA ROSE

season

4

Schitt's Creek Welcomes You To Singles Week

ROSE APOTHECARY

FAN ART BY
JESSICA CRUICKSHANK

SEASON FOUR

Girls' Night

Written by
Michael Short

Directed by
Sturla Gunnarsson

Moira chauffeurs Alexis and Twyla on their girls' night out at a bar, doling out unsolicited romantic advice. Patrick and Stevie push the boundaries of David's ability to compromise. Roland builds a "man cave" in the motel office, forcing Johnny to reconsider Roland's employment.

401

Dead Guy
in Room 4

Written by
Daniel Levy

Directed by
Bruce McCulloch

Moira worries that she's responsible for the death of a motel guest and fears the legal repercussions. Meanwhile, Johnny and Stevie attempt to quietly deal with the removal of the body. Alexis helps Ted interview candidates for the vet clinic, while Patrick and David test the waters of their new relationship.

405

RIP
Moira Rose

Written by
Rupinder Gill

Directed by
Bruce McCulloch

A rumor of Moira's death surfaces online, which puts her in an emotional quandary. Roland asks Johnny to be the godfather to his and Jocelyn's child. David and Alexis go on a buying trip to a local farm, and Alexis realizes that she has an unexpected connection to the farmer.

402

Pregnancy
Test

Written by
David West Read

Directed by
Sturla Gunnarsson

After finding a positive pregnancy test, Johnny and Moira brace themselves for the possibility of a new baby in the family. Alexis struggles with her college enrollment, and David and Patrick search for some privacy.

406

Open Mic

Written by
Daniel Levy and
Rebecca Kohler

Directed by
Bruce McCulloch

Against David's better judgment, Patrick hosts an open mic night to help promote Rose Apothecary. Johnny and Alexis begin rebranding the motel, but Stevie is apprehensive, fearing that they're expanding too quickly. Moira accidentally finds out the gender of the Schitts' baby and tries desperately to keep the secret.

403

Asbestos
Fest

Written by
Monica Heisey

Directed by
Bruce McCulloch

Moira prepares for her headline debut at the annual Schitt's Creek Asbestos Fest, while David deals with a group of loitering teens. Johnny looks to hire new help for the motel and Roland claims to have the perfect man for the job.

407

The
Barbecue

Written by
David West Read

Directed by
Sturla Gunnarsson

Johnny and Moira throw a family barbecue with the intention of getting to know Patrick. But David is worried about inflicting his family on Patrick and tries to keep them apart. Meanwhile, Alexis receives a mysterious text from Ted and, with the help of a new friend, decides to investigate.

408

The Jazzaguy

Written by
Kevin White

Directed by
Sturla Gunnarsson

After the barbecue fiasco, David and Stevie take off on a "romantic" getaway. Johnny steps in at a Jazzagals rehearsal and wows everyone with his skills, but Moira is not fully on board with her husband's new involvement in her social life. Alexis tests out a dating app and goes on a date with a cute local.

409

The Olive Branch

Written by
Rupinder Gill

Directed by
Bruce McCulloch

David finally returns to work, hoping to get back together with Patrick, but learns that he may have left things too late. Moira discourages Alexis from pitching a singles night event at Town Hall, then accidentally finds herself pitching the idea as her own. Johnny buys Stevie a misguided thank-you gift for all of her hard work at the motel.

410

Baby Sprinkle

Written by
David West Read

Directed by
Bruce McCulloch

Alexis runs into her old friend Klair, who offers her an intriguing job opportunity, leading Alexis to take stock of her current situation. Johnny and Moira attend a lock-and-key singles event just to observe, but the matchmaker encourages them to join in. David accepts Jocelyn's desperate plea to plan her baby shower, but aesthetic goals soon collide.

411

The Rollout

Written by
Michael Short

Directed by
Sturla Gunnarsson

Moira tries to get out of jury duty, but when she finds out the nature of the case, her interest is piqued. Johnny blames David's Rose Apothecary products for a rash outbreak at the motel. Alexis runs into Mutt, and their encounter clarifies her feelings for Ted.

412

Singles Week

Written by
Daniel Levy

Directed by
Sturla Gunnarsson

Singles Week gets under way just as Jocelyn's baby arrives, so Moira reluctantly leaves Alexis in charge. Meanwhile, Johnny finally gets Roland to take on more responsibility at the motel, but in doing so he may have inadvertently caused Roland to miss the birth of his child. Patrick takes his relationship with David to the next level.

413

Merry Christmas, Johnny Rose

Written by
Daniel Levy

Directed by
Andrew Cividino and Daniel Levy

It's Christmas Eve and Johnny wants to celebrate with an old-fashioned Rose Christmas party, but the rest of the family has trouble getting into the holiday spirit. Moira brings a negative attitude to Christmas tree shopping, Alexis is already double-booked with another party, and David puts minimal effort into helping with decorations. But the Roses soon realize that the party means more to Johnny than any of them thought.

Behind the Episode

The Number.

CATHERINE O'HARA: The script for "Asbestos Fest" originally had me singing The Number alone, but I asked if I could include David, as if Moira had always coerced David into performing a "party piece" on special occasions. Much to my delight, Daniel played it as if no coercing had been necessary. I wrote a silly Christmas medley in my hotel room with an electric keyboard rented for me by production. I love a good cheesy medley. I sent it to Eugene and Daniel. Caring father that he is, Eugene said it was too much to ask of Daniel, and that he already had more than enough on his plate, but Daniel learned his part in about five minutes and made David a born performer. I love that Dan replicated his hairstyle from The Number in the Christmas episode.

DANIEL LEVY: From the moment we started discussing the idea that David and Moira would do a number at the annual Rose Christmas party, it was something that kind of lingered in the writers' room. It was a funny little bit that we always played around with, but didn't really know where to place it until this episode. Early on in season four, Moira agrees to headline Asbestos Fest, which I think made sense to her at the time because, as we know, she's been involved in so many other philanthropic events, like Artists Against Eczema and the Everybody Nose Benefit for Juvenile Rhinoplasty. But she realizes that she's gotten herself into some hot water. She doesn't know what to do, she panics, she wants to back out. Then David comes in to save the day by offering up The Number.

Originally, we pictured The Number being cabaret style with Moira singing and David accompanying on the piano. Then about a week or so out from shooting, Catherine showed up on set having completely written a holiday medley that was so impressive and yet also so basic. They did a lot of this kind of thing in *A Mighty Wind* and *Best in Show*. It takes a very smart mind to write something so silly. So, I listened to it, and I noticed that it was a duet, and then she tells me, "I just think that David would be singing with her." I panicked because I am not someone who sings publicly a lot, but when Catherine asks, you say yes.

We were really performing it in front of the whole crew. And again, it was another iconic Moira moment. That ultra long wig was a request from Catherine. She loved the idea of a Cher-inspired wig that could also be worn as a scarf that she could toss over her shoulder.

THE NUMBER

conceived by

CATHERINE O'HARA

DAVID   Oh I wonder who that could be!

It's television's Moira Rose!

MOIRA   That's television's "Mom" to you!

You know nothing is colder than the chill I get when I think of the dangers of asbestos poisoning.

Luckily, a little birdie told me, that with enough funds raised, this town could be asbestos-free by...

DAVID   Christmas!

MOIRA   Ding!

DAVID   Dong!

MOIRA   Ding!

DAVID   Dong!

MOIRA   Ding!

DAVID   Dong!

MOIRA   Ding!

DAVID   Dong!

DAVID & MOIRA

On the first day of Christmas my true love gave to me,

MOIRA   . . . the keys to a Lamborghini.

DAVID & MOIRA

Oh come all ye faithful/ Deck the halls with boughs of holly.

DAVID   Yes, I said faithful, which rules out all of you!

DAVID & MOIRA

God rest ye merry gentlemen that nothing you dismay-may-MAAYYY!

THE CAREER HIGHLIGHTS OF MOIRA ROSE

COMPILED BY @SCHITTSSHEETS

Film

DR. CLARA MANDRAKE	**THE CROWS HAVE EYES III: THE CROWENING**
FEMALE BOXER IN GYM	**ROCKY**

Television

VIVIAN BLAKE	**SUNRISE BAY** *(reboot)*
VIVIAN BLAKE	**SUNRISE BAY**
MIRANDA WRIGHT	**MIRANDA RIGHTS**
MARGARET COOPER, PHD	**NOT WITHOUT MY COUSIN** *(Lifetime)*
VARIOUS ROLES	**HALLMARK MOVIES OF THE WEEK**
NURSE 1	**M*A*S*H**
SUSAN B. ANTHONY	**YOU GO, GIRL!** *(pilot for Nickelodeon)*
HOST	**DAYTIME PEOPLE'S CHOICE AWARDS** *(non-televised portion)*

Theater

LADY MACBETH	**"SHAKESPEARE AT SEA WEEK"** *(Crystal Skies Cruises)*
PAULA POKRIFKI	**AN OFFICER AND A GENTLEMAN** *(workshop-only production)*
IMELDA MARCOS	**SHOES, GLORIOUS SHOES: THE IMELDA MARCOS STORY**
MARY KATE CARSON	**TWO HEADS ARE BETTER** *(Foxwood Casino)*
UNDERSTUDY FOR MS. LUPONE	**ONE CRAZY SUMMER: THE PATTY HEARST STORY**
SALLY BOWLES	**CABARET**
LIESL VON TRAPP	**THE SOUND OF MUSIC**
NURSE 1	**HARVEY**
CHORUS	**STARLIGHT EXPRESS**

Miscellaneous

WINNER	**MISS SNOW CONE** *(Barnesville County)*
HAND MODEL	**BI-ANNUAL EAST COAST REGIONAL TRI-STATE MICROWAVE TRADE SHOW**
CENTERFOLD	**SOAP OPERA DIGEST**
VOICE WORK	**MIDORI VINE** *(video game, Japan, rated "M")*
COMMERCIAL WORK	**HERB ERTLINGER WINERY**
	ROSE VIDEO
	ARIGATO ADULT DIAPERS *(Japan)*
	CABBAGE PATCH NATURAL HEARTBURN RELIEF
	LOOKY-LOO BINOCULARS
	S. CREEK TOURISM CAMPAIGN VIDEO

FAN ART BY SARAH FERGUSON

In conversation with

SARAH LEVY *and* **ANNIE MURPHY**

On a beautiful, unlikely friendship.

SL When we meet Twyla for the first time, I don't think anyone would have imagined her and Alexis becoming friends, let alone developing the relationship they ended up having. I think their conversations over the years led them to learn a lot from each other and inevitably to bond. I think Twyla learned from Alexis's confidence, how she leads with her head held high in the world, and how that attitude opens doors for her. For Alexis, I think it's Twyla's self-assurance and humility that rubbed off on her. Whether they realized it or not, they made each other better people.

AM I love the relationship between Twyla and Alexis so much because of how much they help each other grow. It's an unlikely friendship, for sure, especially in the beginning. I think one of their first interactions was Alexis throwing a muffin at Twyla's back to get her attention at the café. They've come such a long way from that moment. By season six, they offer each other a confession of true friendship and a promise that they will visit each other and remain in each other's lives.

SL There were some pivotal moments between them, like when Alexis gives Twyla a heads-up about Mutt planning to break up with her. Considering how empathetic Twyla is toward people in the town, I don't always think she receives that empathy back, and this was such a kind and gentle moment between two women who were in the process of becoming true friends. There's the "Girls Night" episode where you really see the growth in their friendship. They've moved beyond just sitting at that counter. And then there are the scenes from episode 613 when Twyla reveals she's won the lottery and offers Alexis the gift of some money. This isn't just a situational friendship anymore, it's one that's real and lifelong.

AM They really did both take away significant lessons from each other. Twyla's naïvely blunt honesty was very helpful for Alexis. And Twyla observed a lot of Alexis's confidence and took that on for herself. I'm so grateful to the writers for giving these characters such a wonderful, supportive female friendship and allowing it to blossom in front of us throughout the seasons.

BEHIND THE SCENES
Sarah and Annie on location for "Girls' Night."
June 8, 2017

BEHIND THE SCENES
Catherine goofing off while on location for "Girls' Night."
(RIGHT) Annie and the crew in between takes.
June 8, 2017

THE WORLD ACCORDING TO DAVID ROSE

Incorrect

Correct

MOTHS AND BUTTERFLIES

BUGS WITH MILKY EXOSKELETONS

IMPROV

HIGH-THREAD-COUNT SHEETS

EYE CREAM FROM PARIS

LIP BALM

PITTED FRUITS

SLOPPY MOUTHS

HELMETS

RED WINE

WHITE WINE

ROSÉ

BUSINESSWOMEN IN SNEAKERS

TEAM SPORTS

BABIES

MARIAH CAREY

STEVIE BUDD

PATRICK BREWER

BLUE CHEESE

TOILET PLUNGERS

PEAR-SHAPED OPAL RINGS

MALL PRETZELS

COLOGNES THAT SMELL LIKE A FIREPLACE

CARAMEL MACCHIATOS WITH SKIM MILK, TWO SWEETENERS, AND A SPRINKLE OF COCOA POWDER

COMPILED BY @SCHITTSSHEETS

FAN ART BY SUSAN VAN HORN

"Toilet plungers on display at the front of a store is incorrect. Breath mints where the lip balms should be? Not correct. These mountaineering shoes that my boyfriend is wearing, looking like Oprah on a Thanksgiving Day hike? Incorrect!"

DAVID ROSE

Behind the Episode

406 OPEN MIC

Patrick serenades David.

NOAH REID: At the table read for "Open Mic," I remember saying to Dan, "You're going to make me sing, huh?" and he was like, "Yeah, for sure. And that song is very important to me, so don't fuck it up."

He asked me if I wanted help arranging it or if I wanted to take a shot at doing it myself. Dan had actually come to my album release the summer before, so he'd seen me perform live and he knew I could do it. I think that allowed him to afford me a little bit of creative license. Naturally I abused that creative license by taking a really long time to send him anything.

It took me a while to figure out the arrangement, because I wanted to honor the pop drive and rhythm of the song, but also wanted it to be soft and vulnerable and honest, and something that could come from Patrick. Something was happening between those two characters over the course of that performance too, so that moment in the relationship also had to be honored in the performance.

I eventually came up with the arrangement, and I sent it to Dan. I didn't hear back from him for several hours, which is just long enough for the paranoia to creep in. I thought, "Cool, I guess it sucks and I'm probably fired." But Dan says it was just because he was crying alone in his room listening to the recording. So I guess that was good news for me.

When the time came to shoot, I was really nervous to be playing this tune in front of all these people. Guitar is not my A-one instrument, I'm more of a piano guy, so shooting the audience first definitely gave me a couple of free passes to warm up. I think our cast didn't quite know what to expect. The emotional content of that scene caught us all a little bit by surprise.

I also just love the setup of the audience thinking it's going to be terrible, and it turns out to be a beautiful moment of honesty and vulnerability. Just watching David's heart open and watching his mask come down a little bit ends up being a pretty big moment in that relationship and certainly for our audience.

199

Behind the Episode

Simply the best.

KAREN ROBINSON: When I think about my favorite scenes from the show, I keep going back to the open mic night and hearing Patrick sing "Simply the Best" for the first time. I love that scene because the reaction you see from Ronnie and Twyla is absolutely real. You were seeing us hearing that song for the first time. I feel like that song was such an important embodiment of pure, unadulterated love offered to someone else. There was no guile around that. It really just cuts through all of that. You actually got to see the townspeople be swept up and you saw real reactions from the actors playing David, Moira, Twyla, and Ronnie. Everyone watching on set really put any kind of feelings or expectations or judgment aside and simply reacted to "Simply the Best."

CATHERINE O'HARA: Noah's rendition of "Simply the Best," especially with his gorgeous voice, was profoundly beautiful. Then to watch David accept this gift of love was so very touching. From what I knew about David's dating history, it was less than romantic, but here he was, realizing he was truly loved by a wonderful person, a good man. That killed me. I had a hard time not crying and had to turn away from camera a few times to get it together. Both Moira and I were moved to happy tears.

DANIEL LEVY: This was such a pivotal moment, not only for Patrick and David, of course, but also for David and Moira. At one point during the song Moira reaches over to touch David's arm, as if to say, "There's something really special happening here and I'm here with you." I think that subtle physical moment shows so much about the evolving relationship between these two characters, without us ever having to say anything. For us to be able to show this very tender moment between a parent supporting their queer child at one of the most magical times in his life, was a situation that we really wanted to put out into the world.

Behind the Episode

The lost scene.

DANIEL LEVY: More often than not, our episodes would run long and scenes would inevitably need to be cut for the sake of time. In the case of "Open Mic," we shot an additional scene, which was very sweet and funny, and even involved Twyla's improv troop! But when push comes to shove, you have to pick the essential scenes. The ones that are crucial to the storytelling. So, a choice was made to cut that additional scene.

What we didn't anticipate was that somewhere along the line, a still from that deleted scene would find its way onto the internet and cause a fan frenzy. To this day I get messages from people asking to release the scene. Maybe one day. But until that day comes, here are a few more moments to stoke the fire.

THE COMPLETE COLLECTION OF DAVID'S KNITS

DANIEL LEVY: David's sweaters tell interesting stories about his character over the six seasons of our show. During season one he wore a lot more button-up shirts, and his aesthetic was a little more tightly wound. Then over the course of the series, we very consciously unwound him. He stopped wearing button-up shirts and the aesthetic got softer. We were using softer knits, we were using fuzzier textures, anything we could to show that he was becoming more and more comfortable with himself and that he had less and less to prove.

I think one of the first times David ever wore color was in the open mic scene. He was wearing a Givenchy sweater that was black with red and orange flames all over it. We'd had it on a rack and I had always debated if we should use it because of the color. Then the open mic scene came up and I was talking to Debra Hanson about what David should wear. I thought the concept of him choosing to wear color—particularly flames, which in our case represented a love that was being ignited that night—could be symbolic if he inadvertently put on that sweater, not knowing what was to come.

A fun sartorial through-line started with that costume. You have the flame sweater in the open mic scene. Then in the second-to-last episode of the show David is wearing a Dries Van Noten sweatshirt with an open palm on it, which symbolizes openness and honesty, and then in the last scene of that episode, he's wearing an Off-White™ sweatshirt that features a hand with the flame inside. Those were the kinds of details that really excited me. It's been really fun for me to read Twitter threads from fans who have pieced together all of these little subliminal messages. Again, that's the joy of costuming. You get to say things without ever having to write them.

We also really enjoyed finding pieces that literally said something. Be it his "Love Me Tender" sweater in season two or his "Radical Feminist" sweatshirt in season three. I think the first time we saw a message on him might have been in season one— his "Don't" t-shirt, which a lot of people don't know was custom made. Just in case people hadn't gotten the impression that he didn't want to deal with anyone in this town, why not make a t-shirt that really says it out loud?

FAN ART BY HUNTER BARRETT

101

"No, you step aside!"

102

"She would walk into the space wearing a clay mask of a fawn, remove her clothing and breastfeed members of the audience. It was a commentary on income inequality."

103

"Someone's on a health kick, huh?"

105

"Between you and my sister, and the barn guy and that girl in the restaurant, we have five, and obviously we need an even six for ultimate game play."

106

"I'm just not sleeping. And I think there's a lack of oxygen getting to my heart because I'm feeling very suffocated."

107

"I could not be more at one with nature. I do Coachella every year, so . . ."

109

"Hello. Hello. Is anybody in that hollow chest?"

109 & 110

"Walking over to the café and ordering a tuna melt is hardly what I would call a flourishing social life."

111

"The idea of me life coaching another human being should scare you. A lot."

112

"I'm gonna ask you to put some pieces together here for me. We are throwing a 'fund-raiser' that just so happens to be on the same night as your birthday."

113

"Oh, you just watch a season of *Girls* and do the opposite of what they do. It's easy."

201

"Stop saying, 'David'!"

201

"This was before my nose job, how was anyone supposed to recognize me?"

202

"Don't touch me. That's harassment."

202

"I don't know how to fold broken cheese like that!"

203

"How is it that a moth can find its way into a triple-locked titanium suitcase."

203

"I bought a cologne once in Japan that's supposed to smell like the aftermath of a car crashing into a cedar tree."

204

"Yeah, um, in fashion, 'durable' and 'elegant' rarely go hand in hand so . . ."

204

"Oh my god.
You know I have really bad
foot-eye coordination.
You didn't have to wear
corrective leg braces
for three months."

205

"Do you like this sweater?
Jared Leto gave it to me and
I've always been on the fence
about it."

205

"It's a twelve-dollar
negligee on a two-for-one
promotion, so . . ."

206

"Scent is a really
important factor in
defining a brand."

206

"Okay. I am the face of the
company. If I have acne what
does that say about the
legitimacy of the store?"

207

"Now, how diverse is
the clientele at this
local drinkery?"

209

"I don't even wear
good socks in here."

210

"If you find any Xanax
lying around anywhere
can you just let me know
about that?"

211

"There's a collection of
undershirts hang drying outside
of my room. Is there any way
they could be removed or is
there like a *Texas Chainsaw*
movie being filmed out there
that I'm not aware of?"

212

"Something seems
really sketchy about this.
And I'm not just saying that
because I have a hard time
with Australians."

213

"Did he invite you to his
wood shop?"

301

"Excuse me?
I haven't bedazzled anything
since I was twenty-two."

301

"Umm, and I'll have a bowl
of room temperature
hollandaise sauce please."

302

"I'm tasting metal,
for some reason."

302

"What kind of barnyard
were you raised in
where you just eat
someone else's food?"

302

"Let's all be with *us*?"

303

"No used car salesman
is going to cut you a deal
dressed in archival
designer silk."

303

"Uh, tell that to your outfit!"

304

"Do you want my
honest opinion? Or . . ."

304

"Because I was the one
at the consulate sending you
temporary passports and
colored contact lenses
whenever you needed them."

304

"Yeah, I just feel like the whole
session was rushed, like
there was no back lighting, or
emotional direction . . ."

305

"I'm obsessed with this."

305

"They're paying you scale.
But it'll be in Baltic currency.
Do you want me to
keep going?"

306

"Uh, I'm at the buffet and
there is nothing to taste."

307

"I think you're brave!"

307

"Your friends at
Christmas World are looking
for a deeply embittered, mildly
Hebraic-looking elf?"

308

"Ciao. I said ciao,
to that person . . ."

308

"Have you seen
Dad's coasters?"

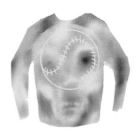

309

"This frame is a little too
corporate for my brand."

309

"He's a business major that
wears straight-legged, mid-
range denim. He's not into me."

310

"I will not feel shame about the
mall pretzels."

310

"Really handsome in like a
homeless-y sort of way. Yes."

311

"What do we think body milk is
if not milk for your body?"

312

"Fortunately, you look like you
have a clean mouth, so . . ."

312

"That kind of language,
folks, will not be tolerated at
Rose Apothecary. Thank you.
This is a safe place."

313

"I plan on popping a pill,
crying a bit and falling
asleep early. So just a
regular weeknight."

313

"A bold claim."

401

"Fall off a bridge, please."

402

"I am not in a place right now to be emotionally available to a baby."

402

"We are getting sidetracked right now, okay, so who is feeling sexy?"

403

"I'm sorry that you connect with a more mature clientele, whereas I vibe with a much younger crowd."

404

"They were fugly brooms with big red handles. They didn't match our sand and stone color palette."

405

"Never say 'nom nom' again."

406

"Okay, no. Worst-case scenario, I watch improv."

406

"A lot of people are shopping, and drinking. I don't even know if we need to do the open mic part."

406

"Okay, have you *ever* gotten an A?"

407

"We're not doing 'Pat.'"

408

"I am suffering romantically right now and there was a minute when I thought I would never have to look at another dating app. And here you are shoving Bumpkins in my face."

408

"Did our waitress just make a sex reference?"

409

"What if I gave you back some of the olive branches that you gave to me?"

410

"What the hell is a 'sprinkle'?"

411

"I just went all Gordon Ramsay on one of my most important vendors. I basically told her her product was like a jar of ebola."

412

"Okay. That compliment could bring me to tears but I'm not gonna let it. So, I would like to thank you for all the wonderful things that you said."

413

"Okay, I just don't know how we're gonna pull this off without the grand piano or the ice sculptures . . ."

413

"I, for one, find it charming, in a sort of war-torn sort of way."

413

"It's like being right back in Japan."

501

"Eat glass."

501

"Okay, you might want to talk to half of my birthright trip about that."

502

"Would we not all agree that words are weapons?"

502

"This is why I think it's best to torch everything from past failed relationships."

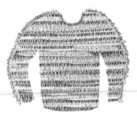

503

"Speaking of size, Ray— I have yet to see a closet. Is there a walk-in that I'm missing?"

503

"Compared to what, a haunted house?"

504

"Keep the mics hot, I'm comin' in."

504

"And those are the shoes we're going with?"

505

"Besides, where are we gonna find a salad bowl of E this last minute?"

506

"We've all been with a handful of other girls, but I'm the only guy."

507

"What can I do to shorten your stay in my store, Roland?"

508

"You asked for my opinion. I don't know how much Romanian marble costs!"

509

"You know my stance on team sports."

510

"Tulips instead of roses—woof."

511

"Okay, what you're dealing with is very personal and it's something you should only do on your own terms."

511

"It was just a very messy day and I was trying to de-tangle things and just make everything okay."

512

"Very impressed. Was not embarrassed at all. And I thought I would be."

513

"I'm not convinced."

513

"I didn't carry you up a mountain not to eat cheese after."

514

"This is not how the announcement was supposed to go."

514

"Jocelyn, I'm the one on the chair!"

601

"I once dated someone who left me for a stuffed animal."

602

"More expensive than my dignity?"

602

"What's the thread count on this plastic?"

603

"You might wanna say hi to Ted. He and Alexis were about to engage in cyber-sex."

603

"'Larry Air' sounds like a dollar-store perfume."

604

"I've thought about it. And I want you to give me away."

605

"Remember that *Waterworld II* premiere?"

605

"Okay, now we're just spiraling off in all directions . . ."

605

"Well, the conversation really ran the gamut. You complimented my flawless skin and called me the Jewish Channing Tatum. Which all tracks."

606

"Jake is nobody's ex and everybody's ex."

607

"Who came up with the word 'bunt.' It sounds like something you'd need to see a surgeon for."

607

"I wonder if that means they'll give you priority boarding when you enter the gateway?"

608

"I want us to look like two very rich people that have just woken up after fainting on a dusty old couch."

608

"I'm practically Sicilian."

609

"Our Lexi's making some wonderful choices."

609

"We won't be doing 'rosy day.'"

609

"Can you stop saying that?"

610

"Might I suggest you explore the duck confit?"

611

"If you're talking about your style, we can bring it back to life—"

611

"I told you I didn't want a jokey bachelor party. Also, my t-shirt is missing the 'with.'"

612

"I thought you'd be excited! Would half a muffin help?"

613

"Wait, one pizza? What is this, *Les Miz*?"

613

"I don't want to be anywhere you don't want to be."

614

"He's a haikuist!"

614

"I just assumed you knew what you were paying for. I was both shocked and impressed."

In conversation with

JOHNNY *and* STEVIE

On a great partnership.

JR   I think we have a very cool relationship. You know, I entered into this relationship actually just to help Stevie out because she was not remotely interested in running the motel and I felt bad for her because, you know, she was just so upset about it.

SB   One time! I was upset one time.

JR   Right, and I wanted to be the nice guy and help you out, which, fortunately for you, I did. The motel is working out quite well and is quite successful, and I think that is due in large part to the great working relationship that Johnny and Stevie have together.

SB   It's a good partnership. I mean it's unfortunate that sometimes we have to bring in other help, like Roland, and that maybe we've made some mistakes along the way, but for the most part I think this business is growing.

JR   And why didn't we put the second *D* on the sign?

SB   Because Alexis said it would look bad.

JR   That's right. Well, we shouldn't have listened to her. No wonder you're pissed off most of the time. We misspelled your name.

SB   You didn't ask me about any of this. But it's okay, I'm doing this for you.

JR   I know, but now I'm thinking it should have been two *D*'s, but it's kind of funny that it's only one. Not only is your name misspelled, it's not even capitalized. It could have been Budrose, which sounds like somebody on a bowling team.

SB   Well, in all honesty, I love the relationship between Stevie and Mr. Rose. I think Stevie needs a father figure and I also think Mr. Rose is looking to be appreciated. I like that. People should ship us on Twitter. You know what that means? That we would be like "Stevohnny."

JR   Yes, well, welcome to the brand-new Rosebud Motel.

SB   Should've had a second *D*.

JR   Or a capital *B*. Nevertheless, quite an honor, huh, Stevie?

Behind the Episode

Majoring in marketing and "pubic" relations.

ANNIE MURPHY: The "pubic relations" scene was hilarious to shoot. I loved watching Eugene, Dan, and Catherine laugh, and having to do take after take, even though it was all at Alexis's expense. That laughter was not forced, they were all really cracking each other up!

    Especially in season four, Alexis really pushed herself to grow in a way that I don't think she would have, had she stayed in LA surrounded by her group of casual acquaintances. I think she was very much formed by her environment, and breaking out of that helped her to realize that she was worth so much more than she thought she was or what she had been told that she was. It took so much courage to do what she did. I mean, she went back to high school at the age of whatever it was, twenty-eight years old? That couldn't have been a comfortable experience, despite her optimistic demeanor. Then she worked to put herself through college. These are all scary and challenging things to do. She could very easily have still relied on her looks and her family, but she chose not to do that. As much as it did break my heart to have to say goodbye to Ted (and to Dustin), to see her go off on her own in the end was the right thing. I'm just so proud of her.

PROP: Alexis's framed diploma from Elmdale College.

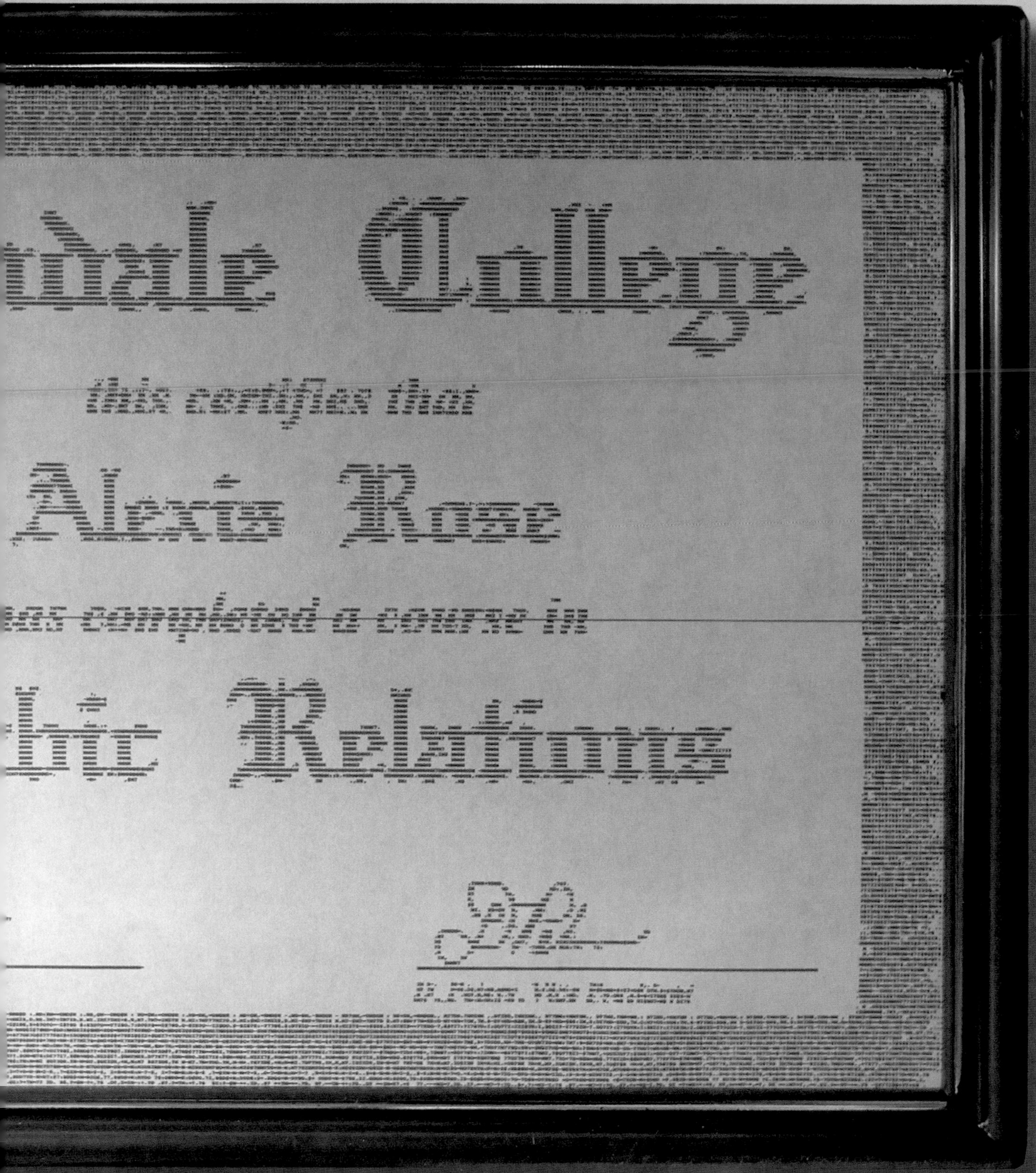
College
this certifies that
Alexis Rose
completed a course in
Relations

Behind the Episode

David serenades Patrick.

DANIEL LEVY: I wrote this lip sync scene into the show and then forgot about it until it was time to shoot. The day before we were set to shoot, I realized that I didn't actually know the lyrics to the song. I knew the chorus, but I definitely didn't know the rest of the words intimately enough to pull off what I wanted to be a really great lip sync. So, I turned it on when I got home from work. I had it on when I cooked dinner. I had it on in the shower. I taped the lyrics to my wall, and it took me all night to learn them, to the point where I didn't really know the lines of dialogue the next day, but I knew the song. On top of that, I'm also not a dancer, and I'm certainly not known for having any kind of smooth moves. On the morning of the shoot I remember thinking, maybe I should have hired a dance teacher!

We were scheduled to shoot the scene after lunch, so I secretly arranged to have a bottle of Prosecco brought onto the set. Noah and I shared the Prosecco and I definitely felt more at ease going into the scene. It was going to be one take with a steadicam, which would be moving around me, and the direction was to just go for it. Not to be concerned with marks, knowing that the camera would catch it. So I just went for it! It was so out of character for me, because I'm not a very expressive person, but I knew that in order to make the scene work, David had to express himself in a way that he had never done before. So, the thrill of me pushing myself way outside of my own comfort zone, knowing it was only going to benefit David's vulnerability, was a very scary and fun thing to do.

The other thing I soon discovered was that I'd been rehearsing to the radio edit of the song, and after minute four of performing, I realized the song just wasn't ending. I tried to keep going with it, but eventually I just kind of fell on the ground and they yelled cut.

When it was over, our director, Bruce McCulloch, came out from behind the set and was crying. My instant reaction was "Oh no, I thought this was supposed to be funny!" Then I noticed that other people were also emotional. And I remember asking him, "Oh god, was that not right?" And he was like, "No, it's a really beautiful scene." It was one of those rare moments where I intended the scene to be a very lighthearted, funny expression of love and I didn't know that it was going to have the kind of emotional impact that it did.

NOAH REID: I've never seen anything quite like Dan lip-synching as David. It might have been the Prosecco we had at lunch, but it seemed like Dan just allowed David to let his guard down and go for it. The best thing was that he had been practicing to the radio edit of the song, but somehow we ended up with the full, uncut version, which was several minutes longer. So there's Dan, half drunk in a leather sweater just giving it his all and wondering if the song would ever end.

THE SCHITT'S CREEK PLAYLIST

COMPILED BY @SCHITTSSHEETS

DANIEL LEVY: The song playing in the final scene of season one as David drives out of town is an Irma Thomas song that I had on my *Schitt's Creek* playlist long before we even finished writing the show. Every season I put a couple songs in a playlist to help inform the tone and to potentially help me visualize moments. That Irma Thomas song, "Live Again," was a really big one because it spoke so clearly to the situation, and in the context of the show it felt kind of heartbreaking, but at the same time it also had a slight element of optimism to it. We actually ended up getting in touch with Irma Thomas to get the rights to the song. I had a full fan freak-out moment over it, and we were fortunate enough to get it. I think that was one of the first licensed songs that we had. We obviously had to be very sparing with the spends on the songs, because our budget was so small, but that was a nonnegotiable one for me. As were "Precious Love" and "The Best."

DO THE DOOT DA DOOT DO *Hollerado* (102)

PARTY POLICE *Alvvays* (105)

LET'S ORDER A PIZZA *Pkew Pkew Pkew* (109)

DANNY BOY *Catherine O'Hara* (109)

GONNA WAIT *The Treasures* (112)

FREE ENERGY *Free Energy* (112)

TENNESSEE WALTZ *Sarah Harmer & Jason Euringer* (112)

STRANGERS IN THE NIGHT *Frank Sinatra* (112)

LIVE AGAIN *Irma Thomas* (113)

DON'T CRY OUT LOUD *Melissa Manchester* (211)

WHICHEVER WAY YOU'LL HAVE IT *New Hands* (213)

LEARN TO LOVE *W. Darling* (213)

SET YOU ON FIRE *Think About Life* (213)

BLUE *Julie Doiron* (213)

THEM KIDS *Sam Roberts* (213)

PRECIOUS LOVE *James Morrison* (213)

ADORE *Amy Shark* (404)

SIMPLY THE BEST *Noah Reid* (406)

THE BEST *Tina Turner* (409)

WHAT I WANTED *Sunlight Project* (412)

EVERY ROSE HAS ITS THORN *Poison* (506)

A LITTLE BIT ALEXIS *Annie Murphy* (508)

MOONLIGHT SERENADE *Glenn Miller* (511)

BRIGHTER THAN SUNSHINE *Aqualung* (511)

TIME AFTER TIME *Chet Baker* (603)

DEDICATED TO THE ONE I LOVE *The Mamas and the Papas* (608)

JESU, JOY OF MAN'S DESIRING *J. S. Bach* (614)

ALWAYS BE MY BABY *Mariah Carey, performed by Noah Reid* (614)

THIS WILL BE OUR YEAR *The Zombies* (614)

FAN ART BY LC MCDONALD

Behind the Episode

Alexis says, "I love you."

DANIEL LEVY: All of our characters have some very tender moments this season, and specifically Alexis has a couple of real doozies. During the shooting of this scene, in particular, we were all sitting behind the monitor watching Annie and everyone was crying. I'm crying. Camera guys are crying. Our director is crying. I turn to my dad and he's sobbing—like couldn't control it, just letting it all out. We're doing take after take; it's free-flowing tears. It's a testament to Annie as an actor and how well she brought this scene to life.

ANNIE MURPHY: This was such a special scene to shoot, and it was so nice to know that Dustin was there in it with me. It was a big moment, because I don't think Alexis had ever experienced love or even friendship. She'd certainly never experienced a state of complete vulnerability. To say "I love you" and not expect anything back was an incredibly sincere and honest moment for her. And then acting to Dustin and a wall of adorable dogs was the icing on the cake.

It was also so nice to know the crew was invested enough in this relationship and in this moment to be having a little cry behind the cameras. I do remember that just after I exited the scene Dustin did a little head tilt, and at the exact same moment one of the dogs also tilted his head. So as I was leaving I heard everyone go, "Aww!" I was like, "I did a great job!" But then I realized it was just the dog completely upstaging me.

Behind the Episode

412 **SINGLES WEEK**

"You're my Mariah Carey."

DANIEL LEVY: David's love of Mariah Carey came from my own personal experiences. I have been a fan since the beginning and her music has helped me through some very precarious times in my life.

Music plays such a formative role in the creative process and in this particular instance, I wanted to honor the artist who helped get me through my teens and twenties, and I wanted to pass that experience on to David.

Having Mariah act as an ongoing representation of love in David and Patrick's relationship was very meaningful to me. So, you can only imagine how meta it all was when she tweeted about that scene. Talk about full circle!

There are moments like this in life when you don't quite understand how all of the pieces came together, but you're so glad they did. I've learned that it's best not to ask questions and just live in the moment as best you can. And I will be living in that moment for quite a while.

BEHIND THE SCENES
Twitter exchange between Mariah Carey and Dan. Otherwise known as:
The Greatest Day of Dan's Life!

In conversation with

CHRIS ELLIOTT *and* JENNIFER ROBERTSON

On the secret to keeping a love life percolating.

CE Right from the start Jenn had a solid take on who Jocelyn was, even while I was still trying to figure out who Roland was, so I just followed her lead. Like the rest of the cast, Jenn fleshed out every detail of her character and I benefited from her diligence because it informed which way I should go with Roland. She totally shaped the eccentric dynamic between the two of them, which was always fun to play, especially when we were around the Roses.

JR Jocelyn and Roland have a lot of fun. They laugh at each other, they love each other, and they don't forget to just have a really good time and accept each other's weird little quirks. And when I say accept each other's, I mean Jocelyn accepting Roland's weird quirks. But let's not forget, Jocelyn will do cartwheels in a thong, so we all have our little things. I think that's what drives them, that they are truly a united couple, and their whole life has been about the town and being important people in that town.

CE One of my favorite scenes was when Jocelyn tells Roland that she's pregnant. We actually had to act with some real emotion in that scene. Jenn nailed it, and I did my best, but it was refreshing that the writers didn't have Roland freak out at the baby news. We had already established that under their quirky facade, Jocelyn and Roland—just like Moira and Johnny—were true soul mates, so Roland could really only react one way, with over-the-top happiness and an eager anticipation for the birth of their sweet little what's-his-name.

JR When it came to having her "miracle baby," Jocelyn just loves Roland so much and I think it's that thing that when you love somebody so much, you're like, "Let's make another person together!" I do think she was excited to have a baby, but she was smart enough to know it wasn't going to be easy. Obviously, as you see in seasons five and six, it really knocked the wind out of her sails. I loved when Dan started talking to me about that for her, because she mostly kept it together for those first few seasons and there's nothing more fun than playing a character that had it all together and watching them fall apart.

Behind the Episode

"I refuse to turn the light off on Christmas again this year."

EUGENE LEVY: As David explains to Stevie in this episode, when she questions why the Roses, a Jewish family, celebrate Christmas, "We're a half-half situation." Johnny was Jewish and Moira was Christian, and the family celebrated both religions. That was the same with the Levys. Daniel knew the fervency I feel for Christmas, and he modeled that fervency for the character of Johnny.

It was important that the audience have a glimpse of what Christmas used to be like in the opulent setting of the Rose family's former life. Contrast this with Christmas since their arrival in Schitt's Creek, when depression overtook the holiday and celebration was put on the back burner. That is, until Johnny dreams of Christmas celebrations past in the mansion, which sparks his idea to throw a Christmas party at the motel. With this scenario in mind, Daniel and the writers set out to harness my own manic insanity about the holiday and lay it on the character of Johnny.

For Johnny, the timing seemed right to once again celebrate the holiday. The family was showing signs of coming out of their doldrums, and they deserved a celebration. The episode touched all the high points of the holiday for Johnny: planning a get-together with family and friends, shopping for the tree, trimming it up, hearing carols sung beautifully by the Jazzagals, feeling a frosty nip in the air, and giving that special gift to a loved one. Or, in Johnny's case in this episode, not quite so special as far as gifts go. Johnny's party, with last-minute help from his family, who knew they had to come through for him, turned out to be a mirror image of his lavish Christmas parties back at the mansion. Minus a few hundred million dollars.

Behind the Episode

413 MERRY CHRISTMAS, JOHNNY ROSE

Building Christmas in July.

DANIEL LEVY: We always wanted to do a holiday episode. In my mind, I thought it might end up being our series finale. But, it ended up as our fourth season finale. It felt like the right time for us to look back at the Roses's old life, reminding our audience just how far they've come.

It was also an opportunity to do some character building with Johnny. My dad often talks about how he's the straight man in the show and how his job is to give others opportunities to be funny. So, it was nice to give him an episode that celebrated both Johnny and Eugene. When the holidays roll around, my dad is the first person to make sure the house is decorated, the gifts are bought and wrapped, and the cookies and candied nuts are out in various bowls around the house. The rest of my family is not quite as festive, but we admire his enthusiasm. This episode is a love letter to my Dad.

When it came to bringing the snow to our often-sunny town, I was skeptical of how we were going to convincingly pull it off. It wasn't until we sat down with the special effects team and were shown all the magic they could create that I began to believe that maybe it was possible. In the end, I was stunned by their work, what they were able to do—adding snow and winter's breath to a balmy summer night shoot, completely transforming the Apothecary into a winter wonderland. Movie Magic was alive and well in that episode and it was such a treat to get to dabble in it for the first time.

The whole production was a group effort. The makeup team did an incredible job of making sure that people's cheeks and noses were nice and rosy. The production design team made sure that the world of Schitt's Creek over the holidays felt charming and nostalgic. Ray selling the Christmas trees out of the barn was a fun and funny touch. And very few things on the show made me laugh quite as much as my dad unraveling that sad tree and it completely falling apart. I think all of us were really trying our best to not fall apart during that scene.

This episode will go down as one of my all-time favorites.

(OPPOSITE) Rosebud Motel before special effects
and Rose Apothecary after special effects.
Eugene and Catherine shooting episode 413, dressed for
snow on a summer night and Ray Butani owning the holidays.

*"We are all on the precipice of greatness
and we must cherish these moments
before everything changes."*

MOIRA ROSE

season

5

A SCHITT'S CREEK MUSICAL
CABARET

FAN ART BY
JESSICA CRUICKSHANK

SEASON FIVE

The Dress

Written by
Rupinder Gill

Directed by
Jordan Canning

Moira's red-carpet gown for the *Crows* movie premiere arrives with a price tag that causes Johnny financial stress. Stevie takes David on a road trip under false pretenses. Ted's old friend from vet school helps out at the clinic, but Alexis feels like she's getting the cold shoulder, and is determined to get to the bottom of it.

501

The Crowening

Written by
Daniel Levy

Directed by
Laurie Lynd

While Moira is in Bosnia filming the *Crows* movie that she hopes will revive her acting career, Johnny digs into work around the motel, and can't seem to slow down. David takes a quiz that suggests he and Patrick are falling into a boring routine, so Alexis encourages David to reinvigorate his relationship by joining her and Ted on an outdoor adventure.

502

Love Letters

Written by
David West Read

Directed by
Laurie Lynd

Back from Bosnia, a sleep-deprived Moira worries about a stack of old love letters addressed to Johnny from another woman. David and Stevie are held up at David's store. Alexis goes to great lengths to retrieve a heart-shaped locket Ted gave her.

503

The Plant

Written by
Rupinder Gill

Directed by
Jordan Canning

Alexis and Johnny hatch a plan to impress a motel reviewer that puts Stevie in a potentially uncomfortable situation. David and Patrick search for a new apartment. Moira helps Jocelyn let off some steam at a Jazzagals rehearsal.

505

House-warming

Written by
Daniel Levy and
Rupinder Gill

Directed by
Laurie Lynd

David and Patrick throw a housewarming party, and Alexis encourages Ted to take a break from work and let loose, but when he does, she immediately regrets it. Johnny wants to prove to Roland and Jocelyn that he and Moira are capable parents, but once he agrees to look after Roland Jr., he's quickly reminded of how tough parenting can be.

506

Rock On!

Written by
David West Read

Directed by
Laurie Lynd

Moira and the Jazzagals take Jocelyn out for a night at the casino. After accidentally walking in on Stevie in her personal space, Johnny attempts to navigate a conversation about intimacy in the workplace. Meanwhile, David emboldens Patrick to go on a date and test an open relationship.

507

A Whisper of Desire

Written by
Michael Short

Directed by
Jordan Canning

Johnny suspects that Ted's mom is attracted to him, but he may have his signals crossed. When Moira hears that Jocelyn is directing a local production of a musical that is close to her heart, she cannot help but insert herself into the action. David is annoyed when he is left to look after Roland Jr. at the store, but soon discovers the perks of fatherhood.

508
The Hospies

Written by
Rupinder Gill

Directed by
Jordan Canning

Johnny and Stevie attend the regional hospitality awards, while Moira does everything in her power to stop Alexis from auditioning for *Cabaret*. Meanwhile, David and Patrick's bathroom renovation is taking longer than expected, and a frustrated Patrick mishandles the situation with Ronnie.

509
The M.V.P.

Written by
David West Read

Directed by
Jordan Canning

Patrick asks David to sub in for the annual Schitt's Creek baseball game, and much to Johnny's delight, David reluctantly agrees. Meanwhile, Moira runs a particularly intense rehearsal for Stevie and the *Cabaret* cast, and Alexis is forced to step in and redirect her mother.

510
Roadkill

Written by
Michael Short

Directed by
Jordan Canning

Johnny and Moira's afternoon plans are interrupted when they hit a cat with their car. David runs into an old colleague at the flea market, but his suspicions are raised when he discovers that she is selling similar products at a competitive price. Ted and Alexis try their romantic role play in David and Patrick's store.

511
Meet the Parents

Written by
Daniel Levy

Directed by
Jordan Canning

David plans a surprise party for Patrick and invites his parents to attend. Johnny and David soon discover Patrick hasn't been entirely truthful with his parents about his life in Schitt's Creek. Alexis drags Moira to a local soap opera convention to make a quick buck. Moira finds the whole experience humiliating, until she sees a familiar face from her soap days.

512
The Roast

Written by
David West Read

Directed by
Laurie Lynd

Johnny volunteers to fill in for Moira at the annual Mayor's Roast, but no one thinks he has the skills to succeed. David distracts Moira with dinner dates to keep her from finding out about Stevie and Patrick's private dance lessons. Meanwhile, Ted suggests that he and Alexis should take a long vacation in the Galapagos, but Alexis is not exactly thrilled with the plan.

513
The Hike

Written by
Daniel Levy

Directed by
Laurie Lynd

Patrick takes David on a long, romantic hike, but David's nonstop fussing starts to ruin the mood. A sudden trip to the emergency room for Johnny sends Moira, Stevie, and Roland into a panic. Ted and Alexis have their tarot cards read by Twyla, who sees something very dark in their future.

514
Life Is a Cabaret

Written by
Daniel Levy

Directed by
Daniel Levy and
Andrew Cividino

It's opening night for *Cabaret,* and Stevie is nowhere to be found, forcing Moira to scramble for a replacement. Meanwhile, David tries to make a big announcement, but keeps getting overshadowed by drama surrounding the musical. Alexis is starting to feel guilty about leaving her family, and Johnny's sentimentality isn't helping.

BEHIND THE SCENES
Catherine as Dr. Clara Mandrake on set for "The Crowening."
March 23, 2018

240

The Crowification of Moira Rose.

CATHERINE O'HARA: For Moira's debut as Dr. Clara Mandrake, I asked Ana Sorys, my hairstylist, if she could style a black wig using Steve Van Zandt's look in *The Sopranos* as inspiration. Ana created something both funnier and more flattering. Lucky Bromhead, our makeup artist, brought in a special effects makeup artist to build me the beginnings of a beak. On the shoot day, Lucky concealed my eyebrows and worked some magic with dark eye shadows. She also played my Bosnian makeup artist in the scene!

ANA SORYS: In preparation for "The Crowening" I had asked Catherine if she had an idea of what she wanted her wig to look like. She said, "You know, I'm thinking it should be a bit of a *Soprano* hairline, slicked back with a devil's peak." So I needed to figure out how to execute that for her. I had a long, black, curly Loretta Lynn wig and I started cutting out alternating wefts. As I kept cutting, getting closer and closer to the scalp, the hair started making a featherlike texture all on its own. I really wasn't sure what the hair was going to do when I started cutting it, so I was very happy that it ended up looking like feathers! I slicked back the top, and when we did the fitting on Catherine, we decided to add a little bit of hair to the widow's peak to give it a bit of texture there.

LUCKY BROMHEAD: I actually played the makeup artist in the scene where Moira is having her makeup done for *The Crowening*. It all started because we knew there would be a makeup scene for Moira, and Catherine said, "Well, can't it just be you?" It was funny because on the day, we were filming in a tiny trailer. There was a camera in there, along with the director and also Eugene reading his lines, because Johnny was supposed to be on the phone with Moira. Catherine kept feeding me lines, but the character of the makeup stylist did not have any dialogue. I was like, "I can't just say stuff!" and she was like, "No, it'll be funny!" It was both a joy and completely terrifying to be in a scene with Moira, but I'm so grateful to have this on-screen memory with her.

For the *Crowening* makeup it was important to all of us that Catherine be still recognizable as Moira. It was a tricky balance, too, because at this point, we're in season five, and Catherine, and Ana, and I, we *know* Moira. We know her, and we love her, and for the whole run of the show, it was important to us that Moira was never a joke. Everything she did was with such intention and seriousness, including this role as Dr. Clara Mandrake. So, we wanted to be able to let Moira (and Catherine) perform without being overwhelmed by a prosthetic.

We came up with the idea to do a baby crow beak, and it was very much a collaboration between Catherine, me, Dan, and effects artist Mark Wotton. There were many conversations about what this woman-crow was going to look like. Moira's character is in a transition phase: she's not fully a crow yet, but she's no longer a woman. It was complicated because if the beak were too big it would take over everything and become comical for the wrong reasons. So, Mark made a few different molds for us to work with. Once we meshed out the beak we were happy with, we realized that she need to look a little bit scary. So, we took out her eyebrows by making them a bit more skin color, because that is another thing that really changes your face, and we made her eyes more beady and black than Moira's normal eyes. But, again, because we still wanted to protect the integrity of Moira and the contours of her face, we kept the shape of her lips and just made them a more neutral color.

Finally, we added talon-like press-on nails. They were gray and we painted the edges black. When Ana put on the wig, it all just came together. To be totally honest, when we looked at Catherine in the mirror we all just died of laughter.

BEHIND THE SCENES
Catherine transforming into Moira as Dr. Clara Mandrake.

Behind the Episode

David on the ropes.

DANIEL LEVY: I instantly regretted writing the ropes course scene. I didn't know exactly how painful it would be to be stuck up there for an entire day, especially considering the setup didn't allow for me to recline or relax on anything, so it was just my arms constantly gripping onto a rope for dear life. But I guess anytime that we can put our cast in a precarious situation, I enjoyed it, and I would do it again in a heartbeat. Seeing Dustin, Noah, and Annie being hauled up into a tree by a crane brought me a tremendous amount of joy.

 After an entire day of clinging for dear life to a wire forty feet in the air, I had the craziest bruises under my arm. I was quite proud of myself in a way. I remember feeling like "this is what being an actor is." By no means was I comparing myself to Daniel Day-Lewis, but I think it's the closest I'll get to method acting.

BEHIND THE SCENES
(TOP) On location for "The Crowening."
(BOTTOM) Dan's photos taken from his perch in the tree.
May 23, 2018

FAN ART BY JESS WATSON

Behind the Episode

The story of The Dress.

How did you find The Dress for this episode?

DEBRA HANSON: The entire episode of "The Dress" was written around a dress reveal, so we knew it had to be something truly worthy of the moment. Dan and I had been searching online retailers for some time, but nothing we were finding felt right. We were starting to become very stressed about it because the episode was coming up. In fact, I had already come across The Dress, a Pamella Roland piece, on a retailer's website, but I put it aside because I knew we couldn't afford it. Then Dan discovered it and sent it to me. I said, "Well, I pulled it, Dan, but it's half the budget of the entire episode!" So, we searched some more, but we both kept coming back to this dress and finally Dan said, "I think we have to have it." The fortunate thing, of course, is that Dan was not only the show runner, creator, director, and actor on the show, he was also a producer. He spoke with the other producers and it was agreed that we could buy the dress if we could also write it into the next season.

This was fantastic news, but when we went to purchase the dress from the department store in New York City, we were told they were restricted from shipping it across the border. They had the dress, they had the size, we now had the budget, but we could not get the piece into Canada. So we worked with the store and agreed that we would fly our buyer, Frances Cabezas Miller, to pick up the dress in New York, which, of course, added to our budget. We found a broker to help us with the customs paperwork and to be on call 24-7 in case Frances was stopped at the border returning to Canada with this magnificent dress. We also had to buy a special suitcase to safely fold the dress into so it could be transported back on the plane.

Because Frances was planning to fly in and out of New York on the same day, she didn't even take a change of clothes. Instead, off she went to New York, with a big empty suitcase, on a mission to pick up the dress. What we didn't know was that she was flying into one of the biggest snowstorms of the season. Her flight into New York was delayed, but the store stayed open late for her. She got there just in time, but then couldn't get out of the city due to the storm. And, so, we had to add a night in a New York City hotel to the budget.

Eventually, Frances and the dress made their way back to Canada, but we still had one final challenge: to fit the dress on Catherine. We'd invested so much in this piece already, and we really didn't have a Plan B, so everything was riding on the fitting working out. Catherine hadn't even seen it yet, but she came in, put it on, and it didn't need a single alteration. It was perfect and, fortunately, Catherine loved it.

For the reprise of the dress in season five we just needed to accessorize a bit, so we added that beautiful headpiece, which was handmade out of gold zip ties.

What was it about this dress that made you sure it would be perfect for the moment?

DEBRA HANSON: What we loved about the dress was the color, the shimmer, and the softness. It was a departure from Moira's usual black and white. It was a beautiful flesh color that we knew, with the addition of Lucky's makeup and Ana's hair, would look fantastic on Catherine. The feathers added a softness to the dress, which was, again, a departure for Moira. This was Moira's big moment to be on the red carpet and we felt she would want to take this opportunity to shine and be beautiful, but also to surprise her fans and turn heads.

We made sure that none of the cast, except for Dan, had seen the dress on Catherine, so when she walked into the motel room to show it off for the first time, the camera is catching a genuine reaction from Annie and Eugene.

BEHIND THE SCENES
Schitt's Creek wardrobe room.
(LEFT) Unwrapping The Dress for the first time.
(RIGHT) Remnants from one of Dan's fittings for David.

In conversation with

DANIEL LEVY

On the importance of authentic style.

DL   I wanted the fashion experience of the show to be real. And I wanted it to be recognizable for people who care about fashion. I wanted fashion people to be able to watch the show and say, "I recognize that archival Balenciaga dress or those Rick Owens boots." That, to me, helps to build a level of authenticity and a level of excitement in the viewer. I always enjoy the experience of feeling like I noticed something that no one else noticed, so being able to build those layers into the show was crucial.

Because our budget was so small, we had to be really thrifty when it came to creating a million-dollar wardrobe on a ten-dollar budget. Unfortunately, the cycle of the show didn't align with sale season, so we were missing out on a lot of opportunities between when we wrapped the show and when we started shooting again. I took it upon myself to buy clothes all year round because without that, it would have been financially impossible to pull off our wardrobes. I scoured thrift shops, eBay, I was on consignment websites, I was going on Black Friday sales. I was doing everything I possibly could to acquire wardrobe for David, Annie, and Catherine. There were times during the year when I had closets stuffed with Moira's dresses. The person taking care of my apartment must have thought I had a way more exciting life than I did!

When shooting rolled around again, I would bring suitcases full of clothes to our first day of pre-production and lay them out with Debra Hanson and the costume team, and we would start to look at what I bought. We tried to plan out certain pieces for certain episodes, but we basically went week by week. We would look at the episode that was coming up and the clothes we had at our disposal, and we would think really hard about why a character would wear what they're wearing. Sometimes it didn't matter. If it was a brief café scene and then there was a wardrobe change, we would probably put on a look that wasn't as flashy, because we had to save those bigger statement looks for the moments when it really counted. Certain situations, like the wedding or "The Dress" episode, obviously required a lot of planning in advance to make sure that we were thinking ahead and we had money put aside.

When it came to Moira's wardrobe in particular, we played a lot with Comme des Garçons, Givenchy, Rick Owens, Gareth Pugh . . . We played with a lot of designers that a lot of people would be too scared to wear because, at times, when the clothes get really directional, there's the danger of the character being worn by the clothes rather than the clothes being worn by the character. It was the greatest exercise ever in playing dress-up.

ALL THE LOOKS OF MOIRA ROSE

DEBRA HANSON: One of the most remarkable things about Catherine is that she can carry anything when it comes to clothes. You can fit a dress on an actor and they will look beautiful, but that doesn't mean they can carry it. That's about having emotional security and presence within the clothes and that's what Catherine has.

#BESTOFMOIRASOUTFITS

In May of 2021 we ran a week-long competition to decide Moira's greatest look. After three rounds and 274,388 votes, Moira's Papal-inspired ensemble from "Happy Ending" was crowned victorious.

HAPPY ENDING

HAPPY ENDING

HAPPY ENDING

SEBASTIEN RAINE

REBOUND

MERRY CHRISTMAS, JOHNNY ROSE

ASBESTOS FEST

THE M.V.P.

FINDING DAVID

HAPPY ENDING

SEBASTIEN RAINE

MERRY CHRISTMAS, JOHNNY ROSE

FINDING DAVID

HAPPY ENDING

HAPPY ENDING

FINDING DAVID

HAPPY ENDING

WINNER

MAID OF HONOUR

THE DRESS

THE DRESS

THE DRESS

MILK MONEY

SMOKE SIGNALS

SMOKE SIGNALS

THE CROWENING

MAID OF HONOUR

LIFE IS A CABARET

THE DRESS

MILK MONEY

RIP MOIRA ROSE

MERRY CHRISTMAS, JOHNNY ROSE

SMOKE SIGNALS

Behind the Episode

Jocelyn's new haircut.

JENNIFER ROBERTSON: This is one of my top favorite moments for Jocelyn, when all the Jazzagals go to the casino and Jocelyn gets that terrible haircut! It took us so long working with Annastasia Cucullo, our hairstylist, to come up with that hair. It turns out a bad haircut that isn't a mullet is a very difficult thing to come up with in a wig version, but we finally got it and it was perfection.

I remember it was a night shoot and we were filming on the school bus. It was one o'clock in the morning, and I had that hair on, and I remember that Sarah was sitting in the seat behind me in that final scene and when I was looking into the compact mirror, I could see her and she said she couldn't stop laughing at the back of my head.

I also really loved that moment for Jocelyn in the casino when Moira gives her that speech about feeling like she's nineteen inside and Jocelyn gives the arms above the head—those sort of triumphant arms.

Moira and Jocelyn's relationship is so great. You're presenting these two ladies in power positions. Typically in screenwriting and TV shows, two women like that would end up fighting each other. It was really important to Dan and Catherine that these two female characters were not combative. Yes, they were very different and there would be misunderstandings, but at no point would the relationship turn into a catfight dynamic, which I so appreciated.

I loved that Jocelyn slowly indoctrinates Moira into the town, and I think Moira's confidence really wore off on Jocelyn. I don't know if they would keep in touch once Moira leaves Schitt's Creek, but there are people that you have in your life for pockets of time that forever change you, and even though you're not regularly in contact with them, you feel that person for the rest of your life, and I think that's what those two characters were for one another.

Behind the Episode

The making of "A Little Bit Alexis."

ANNIE MURPHY: This scene was a real highlight for me. When we were doing the table read, the script said, "Alexis performs 'A Little Bit Alexis.'" I think because I was wildly jealous of Noah Reid and his success with "The Best" the season before, I was like, "Well, I'm just going to write this," not really realizing that Noah is a tremendously talented musician and I am not at all.

Dan shockingly agreed to let me take a stab at it, and so I recruited two of my best friends, who are actual musicians and know what they're doing when it comes to writing music. We holed up in a studio for a couple of days and drank beer and ate pizza while I wrote the lyrics and they did the musician stuff. Out came this song, which I sent to Dan and then held my breath. He wrote back, "I am OBSESSED."

We really wanted this song to be something people would actually listen to. We knew it had to be funny, but we really wanted it to be something that people would perhaps call a guilty pleasure. We succeeded, which is just amazing.

I also choreographed the dance myself, if that's what we want to call it. I made up those so-called dance moves about twenty minutes before we shot. I called Sarah into my trailer, and I was like, "Okay, how is this?" And she was like, "That is so fucking bad and perfect." She was my litmus test, and it went perfectly. I had such a fun time shooting that scene.

BEHIND THE SCENES
The original lyrics for "A Little Bit Alexis," handwritten
by Annie Murphy on a paper plate.

HOW TO BE A LITTLE BIT ALEXIS

FAN ART BY SUSAN VAN HORN

Behind the Episode

509 **THE M.V.P.**

An ode to Noah Reid.

DANIEL LEVY: The baseball episode was written for Noah Reid. Every year Noah hosts a baseball game. I would show up for a sparkling white wine and the spectatorship, but one year I was roped into playing. I hadn't played baseball for probably fifteen years and it was not a great experience for me. I knew I could still hit, but I certainly could not catch, and I walked away from that day thinking that we have to turn this into an episode of the show. So that next year in the writers' room, I brought to the table this idea of a community-based baseball game. The lines were officially blurred between me and David and Noah and Patrick, just in terms of enthusiasm levels and ability, and David West Read's perfect script brought it all together.

I wish that we could have had more time to shoot it. The day we shot that group of scenes, there was the most insane storm approaching and we had a very limited amount of time to get it all done before it just poured. Once it pours on a baseball diamond, you can't keep shooting. You have to call it for the day because of the continuity alone. You can't fake that. We were still packing up the day when the storm hit, but it was meant to be because we managed to get it all done just in time.

BEHIND THE SCENES
Noah and Dan ready to shoot "The M.V.P."
May 28, 2018

Behind the Episode

509 **THE M.V.P.**

"I thought you told me your team was stacked!"

EUGENE LEVY: The idea of spending a day on a baseball diamond and getting paid for it seemed almost too good to be true. So when episode 509, "The M.V.P.," was written, we all knew it was going to be an especially fun day shooting on location. Memories of being in the backyard with twelve-year-old Daniel practicing catching flies and grounders made me think all that practicing might just pay off in this episode. Unfortunately, the episode was meant to highlight how inept David was at the game—a much funnier premise, but a lot of practicing down the drain.

It was comfortable turf for the likes of Noah, quite the athlete in his own right. It was an episode tailor-made for his alter ego, Patrick Brewer, and it showcased his competitive spirit and wanting to win at all costs.

What made it even more extra special was the post-game barbecue that was scripted. It was fun to watch Daniel sneaking hot dogs long before we got to shooting the actual barbecue scene. Storm clouds were rolling in toward the end of the game, and the odds of getting to the barbecue scene were fading fast. We did, however, get to finish the scene and have our hot dogs just before the heavens opened. Through the magic of television, our viewers never saw the drizzle and the umbrellas we were all huddled under as we finished up the scene. It truly was an enjoyable family outing with the largest family of loved ones you could imagine.

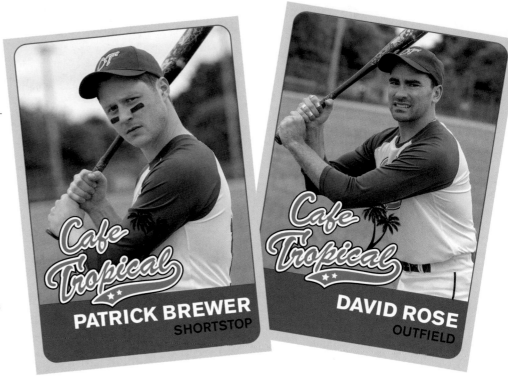

NOAH REID: I host a baseball game every year for my birthday called the Birthday Baseball Classic. Dan has come a couple of times to show off his hitting skills. He's more comfortable at the plate than in the outfield for sure, but I was impressed with his natural batsmanship. I think he went 3–4 with a triple in his first appearance. Shooting the baseball game was definitely one of my favorite days on set: spitting sunflower seeds and chatting with Eugene in the on-deck circle about the Blue Jays. Chris Elliott's seventies-style catcher's uniform was impeccable, too.

I loved the competitive edge that comes up for Patrick in the episode. The Ronnie-Patrick rivalry was so much fun to play with Karen. It always felt like she had the upper hand. Patrick couldn't handle that because he was used to being liked and being in control, but Ronnie just wasn't feeling it. There was a small moment in "Open Mic" when Patrick subtly calls Ronnie out for hoarding drink tickets, and I like to think that's where their rivalry begins. Then

the "he looks like a thumb" insult is probably the highlight of that relationship for me, it's so specific and so terribly accurate.

KAREN ROBINSON: Ronnie takes a journey to include people in her life, and they have to go through a rigorous testing period. I think that is what happened with Moira and I think that is what's happening with Patrick at this point in the season. Patrick has become such an important part of David's life. He could really affect David's trajectory and the way his life progresses from here on in. And I think Ronnie just sees Patrick and goes, "Okay, where are you coming from, and what are you here for? How long do you plan to stay for? What are you going to do while you're here?" I feel like in a way she's protecting David and generally the day-to-day life of this town, because Lord knows if that didn't go well, then the town probably would have imploded.

FAN ART BY KENDALL WISNIEWSKI

Behind the Episode

511 **MEET THE PARENTS**

Patrick comes out to his parents.

DANIEL LEVY: We knew that we wanted David and Patrick to get engaged at the end of season five, but we also knew that they hadn't been through enough hard times to have earned that moment with the audience. We knew there had to be one more moment of major conflict between the two of them that would ultimately bring them even closer and make them ready for the next big step in their relationship.

The only thing we hadn't really explored with Patrick was his family, so that felt like an inevitable place to go. That led to the conversation of whether he was out to his family. What if he's been hiding David from them under false pretenses? But because *Schitt's Creek* was never about homophobia, we had to think about a coming-out story that didn't involve anyone being upset by Patrick's being gay. That led to a long journey of trying to figure out what our coming-out episode was going to look like.

We ultimately settled on this play on fear. What if Patrick had fears about how his parents would react? And then we complicated that idea by having Johnny accidentally let it slip to Patrick's parents and it not go over well. Ultimately, we created an entire storyline around the all-too-familiar potential of them not being accepting. But, because we would never actually show homophobia on the show, we needed to spin that negative into a positive. Revealing in the end

that the reason they didn't react well to the news wasn't about their son being gay, but rather, their disappointment in themselves for not having created a safe enough space for Patrick to feel comfortable enough to tell them.

The minute we came up with that kind of twist, I knew that there was going to be a very meaningful story to be told. I drew on my own experiences and my own irrational fears in those moments, and I remember working on the scene for many nights, really trying to authenticate that moment.

The other interesting thing about this episode is David's reaction to the crisis. He doesn't take well to deceit, but it was important that, in understanding the gravity of Patrick's dilemma, he chose to support his partner. This episode felt like a very big turning point in David's life. One where he instinctively knew "now's not the time to make this about me." This felt like a really lovely new side to the character that we had never seen before.

I think that whenever you tell a story that is so personal to so many people, it's crucial that it doesn't trivialize, minimize, reduce, or soften the edges of that experience, but instead celebrates what it is to be accepted in arguably one of the most vulnerable moments of your whole life. It's been so gratifying to hear how affected people were by it.

NOAH REID: I was quite nervous to shoot the scenes for "Meet the Parents." I felt this pressure to get it right, knowing what an important moment this was for Patrick and also for our audience, especially our fans in the LGBTQIA+ community. As a straight guy, I didn't want to misrepresent the moment or get it wrong somehow. But then I thought, if I'm feeling this pressure over a fictional scene in a television show, imagine what it would be like to be in Patrick's shoes right now, about to tell your parents, who have raised you and supposedly know you better than anyone, that there's an essential element of your identity that they don't know. The stakes are incredibly high. There's a fear that they might be angry or upset, that they might think of you differently, that they might not love you the same way. I never had to come out to my parents, and I don't think I had fully considered what that would be like until we shot that scene. It's a moment that requires so much bravery and so much trust, and I'm very grateful to have been a part of a coming-out story that exemplifies love, support, and understanding, all with a beautifully light comedic touch and an emphasis on the humanity of the situation. I think this is probably the best-written episode of the series, but maybe I'm biased.

511

7   INT. PATRICK'S APARTMENT - DAY   7

David lets himself in, carrying a bouquet of flowers and a   *
pizza box. Patrick, touched, tries to take them from him.   *

                    DAVID
          Happy Birthday. The flowers are for
          you. The pizza is my lunch.

                    PATRICK
          Thank you. How's the store?

                    DAVID
          Thriving. How are you, more
          importantly? Getting lots of calls
          from friends and family?

                    PATRICK
          My parents called earlier. They're
          on a little weekend getaway so they
          couldn't talk for long.

                    DAVID
          That's nice. Did you tell them
          about dinner tonight?

                    PATRICK
          Uh... they were just pulling up to
          their hotel so they had to jump
          off. Why do you ask?

                    DAVID
          You know, speaking of your parents,   *
          I just realized I've never spoken   *
          to them outside of work.   *

                    PATRICK
          Okay... I'm sure you have.

                    DAVID
          ~~Yeah, like~~, they know about me,
          right?

                    PATRICK
          Of course they know about you. Why are you asking this?

                    DAVID
          Like they know about us, right?   *

                    PATRICK
           (deep inhale)
          Okay, David. I've been wanting to   *
          tell them about us.

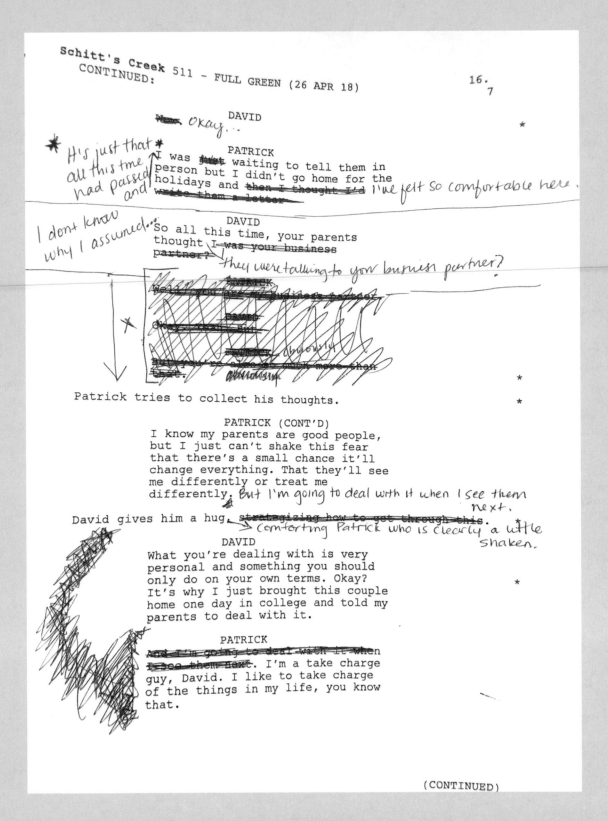

DAVID
~~Now~~ Okay...

It's just that all this time had passed and

PATRICK
I was ~~just~~ waiting to tell them in
person but I didn't go home for the
holidays and ~~then I thought I'd~~ I've felt so comfortable here.
~~write them a letter~~

DAVID
I don't know why I assumed... So all this time, your parents
thought ~~I was your business~~
~~partner?~~ *they were talking to your business partner?*

~~PATRICK~~
~~Well you're not my business partner~~

~~DAVID~~
~~Okay, Patrick, I'm~~

~~PATRICK~~
~~No, you're so much more than~~ *obviously*
~~that.~~ ~~obviously~~

Patrick tries to collect his thoughts.

PATRICK (CONT'D)
I know my parents are good people,
but I just can't shake this fear
that there's a small chance it'll
change everything. That they'll see
me differently or treat me
differently. *But I'm going to deal with it when I see them next.*

David gives him a hug, ~~strategizing how to get through this.~~
→ Comforting Patrick who is clearly a little shaken.

DAVID
What you're dealing with is very
personal and something you should
only do on your own terms. Okay?
It's why I just brought this couple
home one day in college and told my
parents to deal with it.

PATRICK
~~And I'm going to deal with it when~~
~~I see them next.~~ I'm a take charge
guy, David. I like to take charge
of the things in my life, you know
that.

(CONTINUED)

BEHIND THE SCENES
Dan's original script for "Meet the Parents," including his last-minute revisions and annotations.
April 26, 2018

271

BEHIND THE SCENES
(RIGHT) A letter of gratitude from Serendipitydodah for Moms—Home of the Mama Bears,
an organization dedicated to supporting families with LGBTQ members, signed by more than
1,800 members and sent to the cast and crew of *Schitt's Creek*.

Serendipitydodah for Moms

May 20, 2019

Dear Mr. Dan Levy, and cast, crew and writers of Schitt's Creek,

We belong to a large private Facebook group called *Serendipitydodah for Moms - Home of the Mama Bears*. The group was created for moms of LGBTQ kids who love and support their kids. We have more than 5,000 moms in the group and many of us are working to make the world a kinder, safer, more loving place for all LGBTQ people to live.

More than 1,800 of us are signing this letter because we wanted to say thank you for the LGBTQ characters, relationships and story lines that you have included in Schitt's Creek. Your commitment to represent love and tolerance in your show is so important to families like ours.

Your willingness to explore, inform and educate about LGBTQ people and their relationships in an entertaining but respectful and positive manner sets a tone that is often missing.

We have noticed and appreciated the way you focus carefully on important details. Your sensitivity and concern are apparent, and it means a lot to us. The way David and Patrick's individual characters and relationship has developed has been outstanding and caused us to fall in love with them. You have created new ways for queer viewers to see themselves represented and in its own way that is just as important as the battles we are still fighting. Therefore, the work you have all done on Schitt's Creek has encouraged us greatly and given us much hope about the future for our kids.

We sincerely believe that shows like Schitt's Creek will serve as a catalyst to help change the world into a kinder, safer, more loving place for all LGBTQ people to live and because of that we will remain forever grateful.

Thank you for everything each of you brought to the project. You have made a lot of Mama Bears happy and as a result you have a whole bunch of forever fans.

With sincere gratitude and respect,

Behind the Episode

Four gold rings.

DANIEL LEVY: Early on when we started to play with the idea of David and Patrick getting engaged and then ultimately getting married, I was lying in bed one night and it came to me: Patrick would propose with four gold rings exactly like David's set of Margiela silver rings. I kept that thought locked away in my brain until it was time to start writing that episode.

I spent a lot of time, especially falling asleep at night, thinking about these kinds of details. I think when you're making a television show that you know people are enjoying, it feels important and almost necessary to include your audience; to give them Easter eggs that help them feel connected to us and us to them. I knew that so much of what made the show special was those little details.

Patrick proposing with four gold rings was also very revealing of his character. He knew how perfect those rings would be for David. It was a beautiful reminder that David had found someone who really understood him for everything he was and that these two were on the right path.

BEHIND THE SCENES
Dan and Noah shooting the engagement scene for "The Hike."
May 24, 2018

BUILDING THE SHOW WITHIN THE SHOW

DANIEL LEVY: *Cabaret* felt like such a Moira Rose production. There was drama, intrigue, politics, glamor, outfits, artistry, and legacy. It also made sense that it had been her first big starring role. We could totally see Moira Rose as Sally Bowles.

It was quite an experience putting that entire production together. Fortunately, David West Read was a Broadway playwright, so we turned to him for help and guidance throughout the episode. I directed with Andrew Cividino and I think it was some of the most beautiful cinematography we've ever done on the show. It was one thing to write it, it was quite another thing to realize, oh we actually have to *stage this entire thing*. We have to figure out what the sets look like. We have to train our actors to do these numbers. We have to work out production design and lighting schemes. It was a full-on thing, and on top of that it was important to me that the show be a success for Moira. After all these years of hearing about all the shows she's been a part of, but never actually seeing them, we wanted to surprise the audience with Moira's capabilities. We really wanted the unexpected twist to be that Moira is incredibly capable and that her experience, her travels, and her love of fashion, art, and culture would prove authentic. Moira deserved that win, and the audience deserved to take Moira seriously. In creating the production, we were always riding that fine line between making it look too professional but also not have it look like a joke. We had to find that essence of good regional theater.

The result was truly extraordinary. I've always loved those big moments, when the show got to call on and celebrate the talents of the entire team. Like Patrick and David's wedding, *Cabaret* was an expression of every department: hair, makeup, costume, lighting, photography, acting, singing, writing, dancing. It was amazing. Everyone knocked it out of the park.

Then of course you had Emily's number, which I know she had worked so hard on. We didn't even need to do anything. We just needed to put the cameras in the right spot and record it, because what she did on that stage was so beautiful, mesmerizing, and heartbreaking.

"Maybe this time I'll win!"

EMILY HAMPSHIRE: I remember when Dan was writing season five and he said to me at one point, "This is Stevie's season," and I didn't exactly know what he meant by that. When he told me that we were doing *Cabaret* I was so excited. My dream role from when I was younger was always to play Sally Bowles in *Cabaret*. As an actor, that's my absolute. If I could do any role, it would be that. I never in a million years thought Stevie would be the lead. I always thought if we did a musical, Stevie would be the background person in black who comes and sweeps the stage or something. And then to read it and find out that Stevie is Sally Bowles, it was this meta meta dream come true for me.

But then I realized that Dan gave me the even bigger dream that I didn't even know I wanted, which was to play Sally Bowles *as* Stevie. The reason I love *Cabaret* is because Sally Bowles doesn't have to be the greatest singer and the greatest dancer, and I know I'm not the greatest singer and I'm *definitely* not the greatest dancer, so that part always felt right for me. But playing the role as Stevie felt even more right.

When Stevie gets to sing "Maybe this time I'll win," maybe this time I will be as great as everybody around me thinks I can be, and maybe I really do have it in me, it's this moment that is so empowering. And in a way there was a lot riding on it for me as an actor because I really wanted to take any kind of actor ego out of it. I didn't want it to be about Stevie performing well. I really wanted it to say something for Stevie that she couldn't say. For her to lose herself in that moment and speak in a way that she couldn't otherwise speak. For Stevie to even say those thoughts out loud, like "maybe I'm good enough," that's what I wanted for her.

I also remember being adamant that I wanted it to be done live. Like everything in *Schitt's Creek,* it should be honest. Luckily, Dan, of course, wanted the same thing. It was a big moment for me and a big part of it was hearing David say, "That's my friend!" That was the greatest thing ever.

Behind the Episode

"I showed up to our first rehearsal in jeans."

NOAH REID: *Cabaret* was a serious endeavor. I am not a natural dancer, but I do a lot of theater and have a sense of comfort on stage. The Emcee is such an iconic part, and so different from what I normally get to do, so I was excited for it. I also thought Patrick's probably not the world's best dancer, so you know, whatever it is will be fine. Emily and I were equally struggling to keep up with the choreography, which was comforting. I showed up to our first rehearsal in jeans, which is a total rookie move, and then somehow refused to learn my lesson and just kept doing it. But by the time we got around to shooting those sequences, we had a real sense of accomplishment, which is probably how Patrick and Stevie would feel—outside of their comfort zones in that way, but still feeling like they had done something they could be proud of.

I remember we were filming in Theatre Passe Muraille in Toronto, which is one of the only theaters in Toronto I hadn't worked at, and it's a great little space with this beautiful balcony upstairs. The entire cast was there that day. It felt like we were in a Robert Altman film or something, backstage scenes and people coming in and out. We didn't have a ton of time, so there was this great live performance "now or never" kind of energy in the building. We had to do "Willkommen" in, like, three takes at the end of the day, and we all sort of banded together like a community theater cast would. We could feel the support of our castmates out there in the audience, too. I remember people kept saying, "Don't worry, if we can't get a clean live vocal, we can do it in post-production." And I was like, "No way, man, we're getting this. We're getting a live take. We got this." It was hard to hit some of those notes and harmonies while carrying out that choreography, but we did. I'm very proud of all of us for that, and really thankful for the dancers in that number who elevated the whole thing and helped us through. I also loved walking down the street to have lunch in a nearby park in our full *Cabaret* costumes. People must have thought we were nuts.

BEHIND THE SCENES
The cast of *Cabaret*, banding together before their live performance.
June 13, 2018

BEHIND THE SCENES
Emily and Catherine filming Moira's pep talk scene in episode 514, "Life is a Cabaret." June 13, 2018
(LEFT) Catherine, Noah, Annie, and Sarah.

*"Our lives are like little bébé crows carried
upon a curious wind. And all we can wish,
for our families, for those we love,
is that that wind will eventually
place us on solid ground."*

MOIRA ROSE

season

6

FAN ART BY JESSICA CRUICKSHANK

SEASON SIX

601
Smoke Signals

Written by
Daniel Levy

Directed by
Daniel Levy

David and Patrick scout a potential wedding venue on their way to drop off Alexis at the airport, while Johnny and Moira have a romantic picnic by the creek.

602
The Incident

Written by
Daniel Levy

Directed by
Jordan Canning

David is embarrassed by a childhood issue that resurfaces. Johnny, Stevie, and Roland attend a viewing at a motel nearby. Alexis helps Moira join social media. At first resistant, once she gets the hang of it, Moira can't seem to get enough.

603
The Job Interview

Written by
Michael Short

Directed by
Andrew Cividino

Johnny and Moira endeavor to secure an investor for a new motel. Alexis and Ted struggle with maintaining a relationship long-distance. David helps Stevie with a job interview for a local airline.

604
Maid of Honour

Written by
Kurt Smeaton

Directed by
Andrew Cividino

After Moira shares the newly released *Crows* movie trailer with the Jazzagals, she can't help but notice Jocelyn's lack of praise. Johnny and Roland find a suspicious bag of money at the new motel and organize a stakeout to get to the bottom of it. David chooses his maid of honor.

605
The Premiere

Written by
David West Read

Directed by
Andrew Cividino

Alexis plans a local premiere for the *Crows* movie and everyone in town wants to make an appearance on the red carpet. David tends to Patrick after getting his wisdom teeth removed, and Patrick announces some unexpected ideas for their future. After her short-lived stint with Larry Air, Stevie makes a big career decision.

606
The Wingman

Written by
David West Read

Directed by
Donna Croce

The video from the *Crows* premiere goes viral, thrusting Moira back in the public eye and flooding Alexis with attention. Johnny helps Bob get back out in the dating world by taking him for a night out on the town. David and Patrick contemplate an offer from David's old flame Jake.

607
Moira Rosé

Written by
David West Read

Directed by
Jordan Canning

David helps Moira sample wine at Herb Ertlinger's vineyard for her new label, while Johnny attempts to have "the talk" with Patrick. Alexis brings Stevie, Twyla, Ronnie, and Jocelyn to an unusual fitness class.

608

The Presidential Suite

Written by
David West Read

Directed by
Andrew Cividino

Johnny and Moira treat themselves to a night in the Presidential Suite at the new motel, but soon discover that Jocelyn and Roland had the same idea. Alexis is pleasantly surprised by a visitor but struggles with the news he brings. David and Patrick ready themselves for their engagement photo shoot.

609

Rebound

Written by
Michael Short

Directed by
Jordan Canning

Johnny becomes overly involved in Alexis's romantic life. Moira learns she offended the townspeople and must make amends. Jocelyn helps out David and Patrick at the store, and much to David's annoyance, she's a top-notch salesperson.

610

Sunrise, Sunset

Written by
Kurt Smeaton and
Winter Tekenos-Levy

Directed by
Jordan Canning

Moira's former *Sunrise Bay* producers show up with big news. Alexis binge-watches old episodes and gives Moira advice on how to negotiate. Meanwhile, the new motel is proving to be a money pit for Johnny, who is worried about paying for David's lavish catering bill for the wedding.

611

The Bachelor Party

Written by
David West Read

Directed by
Andrew Cividino

The Roses gamely attend David and Patrick's bachelor party at an escape room, but their enthusiasm wanes the more their personal dilemmas come to a head. Johnny anxiously awaits an important business call, Alexis questions her future, and Moira second-guesses her decision about the *Sunrise Bay* reboot.

612

The Pitch

Written by
Daniel Levy

Directed by
Andrew Cividino

Johnny, Stevie, and Roland head to New York to pitch their business idea, while the family anxiously awaits their return. Alexis and David get ahead of themselves and contemplate living in New York.

613

Start Spreading the News

Written by
Daniel Levy

Directed by
Jordan Canning

Johnny celebrates his big win, and Moira receives some unexpected news that alters their plans. David makes a decision about where he wants to live, and it comes as a surprise to the family. Alexis and Twyla engage in an emotional gift exchange.

614

Happy Ending

Written by
Daniel Levy

Directed by
Andrew Cividino
and Daniel Levy

David is stressed out about the rain on his wedding day, so Patrick gets David a massage to help him relax. Meanwhile, Johnny scrambles to find a new venue, Alexis is embarrassed by a wardrobe oversight, and Moira takes on the role of officiant.

BEHIND THE SCENES
The first table read for season six.
March 29, 2019

WRITING A HAPPY ENDING

DANIEL LEVY: I originally thought we were going to end the show after season five, but then we were offered two more seasons instead of one, which allowed us to really take our time over twenty-eight episodes to wrap things up. To be perfectly honest, we needed that time. We didn't want everything to feel backloaded in a rush to end our stories. With the additional season we could take our time with each character and bring each storyline to a meaningful and satisfying conclusion. With that in mind, we began a two-season journey of figuring out how our story was going to end. Or at least how we were going to say goodbye to our audience. And I knew that we had the best writing team in place to figure that out. David West Read, Rupinder Gill, and Mike Short had been with the show for many years, in Mike's case, from the very beginning, and I can't express how reassuring it was to navigate this last chapter with them.

It was a strange day to post the announcement that the show was ending, because it felt at the time like, "Well, we can't go back on it once it's out there!" I knew it was coming for a year, but I never really imagined the day that it was going to happen. I am perpetually impressed by the grace of our fans because, while they were quite upset and saddened by the news, there was this positive sentiment of "we understand."

The fans of the show have created such a safe space for each other on the internet. I think because the show is quite hopeful, many fans who have gone through personal tragedies or have hit any kind of speed bump in their lives have found support and a sense of community through the fandom, which is so amazing to see.

For me, the show has always come first. Making sure that we were continually striving to put out the best possible season that we could. That we were telling the most compelling stories, challenging our actors, and always evolving our characters. I always knew that the minute I felt adding another season would change that process, it would be time to end the show. As a writers' room, we had known how each character would say goodbye for quite some time. And this really felt like the inevitable last chapter in the story of this family and this town. It just felt right.

Behind the Episode

Roland to the rescue.

CHRIS ELLIOTT: It's amazing to watch Catherine work because she loves to try out lots of different things. She comes from the SCTV school where the creative process was very collaborative, and so she was always open to input from fellow cast members and crew members alike. She frequently saved my ass when I was struggling with a line, and I grew to rely on her guidance. Besides being a great actor, she's also a master of physical comedy, which I love. My favorite scene to shoot with Catherine was when the Roses' motel room catches fire and Roland runs in and throws Moira over his shoulder and rescues her . . . and then, at her demand, runs back in and rescues her wigs. We shot that scene several times and Catherine was so concerned that I was going to hurt my back, but she was light as a feather, and I was having so much fun, I could have done it at least ten more times.

ANA SORYS: One thing that people might not know is that in episode 601 "Smoke Signals," when Moira is trying to save her wigs from the fire, the names she's calling out are actually the names of some of her good friends. She named her wigs after them!

FAN ART BY CHRIS ABLES

"My girls! Lorna! Second from the left.
If she takes on smoke, she'll never recover."

MOIRA ROSE

CATHERINE O'HARA: I love that Moira got to have this thing where she wears wigs all the time—wigs with names, no less. Production had a lot of questions about when she was going to wear them, and would they match the wardrobe? And I was saying, "No, we can't lock it down. It has to be on a whim. Sometimes I'll be depressed and wear a dreary, colorless thing. Sometimes I'll just want to look great. It all depends on what's happening internally, and I don't want to have to decide anything in advance!" So, I was already taking Moira's wigs very personally and, I'm embarrassed to admit, I was not really considering what I was asking of our hairstylist. Thankfully, she was more than up to the challenge and, again, the outcome was even better than I imagined. Ana Sorys and I had such fun brainstorming hair ideas which she then brought to life. We had so many great laughs trying out looks, turning wigs sideways and backward, putting wigs on top of wigs, and making a beautiful fool out of Moira. It's a wonderful thing to be able to collaborate with people who are not only extremely talented, but also have a great sense of humor.

ANA SORYS: For Catherine, wearing a wig was more of a mood and a feeling than a look. I would show up each season with more wigs than the season before. By season six I was bringing in twenty-four wigs. Catherine almost never planned her wigs ahead of time. When she changed into her wardrobe and was about to go onto set, she would pick a wig and be like, "Okay, this is what I'm in the mood for." She wouldn't match her hair to her wardrobe, but sometimes she would have a specific idea in her head, and sometimes I would have to adjust or alter the wig for her on the fly to get it to do what she envisioned.

A lot of the wigs were custom, of course. I would add extensions to them or I would cut them and color them according to what I thought she might be looking for and because I wanted the hair to be flattering for Catherine's face. With the exception of a few wigs like "The Crowening" and the wedding wig where we collaborated ahead of time, she really didn't prep with me. I just made sure to have all of the wigs on hand, and we would go from there.

THE COMPLETE COLLECTION OF MOIRA'S WIGS

DANIEL LEVY: One of the first character ideas that Catherine brought to the table was this idea that Moira would use wigs both as a form of self-expression and as a coping mechanism. I remember thinking that felt like a really ambitious thing to keep up for six seasons, but you trust Catherine when she comes with something like that. Anything you think you know, you put aside and trust that she has a bigger picture for what she is bringing to the table, and so we facilitated whatever wigs she wanted. Every year I would say to Ana, "Just make sure that we have enough wigs for Catherine." I never wanted Catherine to be without a wig. So, Ana would go spend the year collecting wigs.

In the beginning, I tried to help preplan the wig to the outfit, but Catherine was insistent: It wasn't an aesthetic thing. It's an emotional thing, so sometimes the wig will not match the outfit. And she'd really manipulate those wigs. She'd take them to places I never knew a wig could go!

FAN ART BY HUNTER BARRETT

294

102

"So, Jocelyn. You said you teach high school? Or you want to finish high school? I'm not sure, I couldn't hear over your husband's chewing."

103

"They're no-name commenters. Tormentors. Anonymous. Ominous."

106

"It's fruit wine, what's not to like?"

107

"I can't tell you how freeing it is, Jocelyn, to try something new like this."

109

"Oh, Danny boy, the pipes, the pipes are calling."

110

"What if I didn't ask 'Who's the eyebrows buying everyone's drinks?'"

111

"If you mention pork one more time . . ."

112

"Never in the history of surprises has one been so delightfully blindsided."

113

"There are certain things that are just not done. Smoking in a car with a baby, unless you crack a window. Tipping before tax. Mixing drinks with cola. And giving away a coat that doesn't belong to you."

201

"I was worried sick, dear. 'Where's David? Or his bags?'"

203

"Why don't we reschedule this for two weeks from now when you're all more prepared?"

204

"Poor dear. Enchanted by a deathbed."

207

"Trying to get council to focus on the simplest things is like . . . wrangling monkeys."

208

"Color me impressed."

210

"Needless to say, that was the last time I played charades with Fran Lebowitz."

212

"Oh, John. What have I done?"

213

"Sort of a *Lady and the Tramp* meets *9 ½ Weeks* dinner date?"

301

"One might think that an additional thirty minutes will make no impact, but you tell that to the mother whose manicurist just applied the wrong color and must start all over again. Or the father who got stuck in a mine."

302

"Is it a crime, Alexis, that I had so many queries for you that I wrote them down in anticipation of forgetting them?"

303

"I apprenticed costume design under Stan LaCoulier. I'm sure he'd agree this toggery is the perfect tribute to the common woman."

305

"Okay, David,
I'll need you to
count me in."

306

"You are bored, lethargic,
and practically dripping
with ennui."

310

"There is a big fat line
between charm and
bullshit."

311

"I won't be pitied, John!
Or fed your pacifying pablum
like some kind of
soft-headed infant."

313

"Baby, I'm yours."

403

"There is an elephant
in the room, David, and he's
whispering 'retire.'"

403

"That's television's 'Mom'
to you."

404

"Gossip is the devil's
telephone. Best to just
hang up."

404

"It took a year . . .
but if it's meant to be,
they'll come around!"

405

"Honestly, what kind of
kitten befriends
a giraffe?"

406

"Why isn't it just Rose Motel?
The Rosebud makes it a
sad stunted thing."

407

"Well, let's hope that
you continue to surprise
each other. It keeps the
relationship titillating."

408

"Oh, there's so much time
wasted off top, John.
Yap, yap, yap, do, re, mi.
And lip buzzing 'til I'm
blue in the face!"

411

"Jocelyn, you're about to
witness a master class in
judicatory persuasion."

413

"Paul Shaffer,
you are my most
cherished friend."

413

"Oh, Jocelyn, surely the
dentures have been dropped
in the glass by now."

501

"In terms of my eyeline,
how many birds am I clocking?
And, of them, how many
are mutants?"

502

"Caw!"
(unintelligible Bosnian)

505

"Seriously . . . a nighttime
couples massage?
What is this, 1985?"

506

"Excuse me, Emilio! Pause.
That kind of physical touch
is inapprop-ri-rate."

506

"Yes, why not throw caution
and the dress code
to the wind?"

509

"I'm 100% confident that
you will all soon see what
I hope I believe I may be
seeing in you, Stevie."

511

"Happy
birthday!"

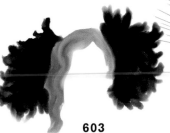

512

"David, full disclosure,
you have been awfully
clingy of late."

514

"Unfortunately, I have no
choice. So I'm going to shimmy
off the rust, and pray there's
still dazzle within."

601

"John, remind me to
reprimand that latch,
it's been awfully
moody today."

602

"Speaking of yummy
opportunities. John, were you
able to return Bill and Melinda's
call today about the hmm hmm-
hmm?"

603

"No, we must keep the
carriage in the wake
of the mare."

605

"Alexis, Mommy's home now.
I'll take it from here."

607

"What do we have here?
I seem to have stumbled
into some sort of
gentlemen's cavern."

609

"You are blessed with
anonymity, and thus will never
have to know the crippling fear
that accompanies
global repute."

609

"Won't you join me for a
little stroll through the slice
of paradise I like to call . . .
the town where I
currently am?"

610

"This doctor would rather nurse
her potable, if you don't mind.
Best to stay lucid for
our congress."

611

"You know what they say.
When one door closes,
the floodgates open."

611

"I thought there were
drinks? "

611

"Jocelyn, are we now
moonlighting as
town crier?"

613

"Worry is but
undernourished
enthusiasm."

614

"Is it David? Did he say
something to upset you?
He can be very cruel,
but it's all fear-based, dear,
so please don't take it
personally."

614

"We are gathered here today
to celebrate the love between
two people whose lives were
ostensibly brought together
by the fated flap of a
butterfly wing."

BEHIND THE SCENES
(ABOVE) Catherine and Ana playing around with wigs after
shooting "The Bachelor Party." June 19, 2019
(LEFT) Ana Sorys grooming Moira's wigs. May 3, 2019

Behind the Episode

601 **SMOKE SIGNALS**

Johnny and Moira: A love story.

EUGENE LEVY: Johnny and Moira is the love story that has stood the test of time. From "Who's the eyebrows buying everyone's drinks?" to "It was worth the wait," it was apparent to both of them that they were meant for each other. Moira is the color and the fun that Johnny needs in his life and Johnny is the solid-as-a-rock stability that is sorely lacking in hers. The scales here are perfectly balanced and this is the cornerstone of their successful marriage. Without Johnny, there is no question Moira would not have survived in Schitt's Creek. And Johnny, in the marathon that was shaping the future of his family, would never have made it to the finish line in Schitt's Creek without Moira.

BEHIND THE SCENES
Eugene and Catherine on location for "Smoke Signals."
June 12, 2019

BEHIND THE SCENES
Dan on location directing "Smoke Signals."
(RIGHT) Catherine on location shooting "Smoke Signals." June 12, 2019

BEHIND THE SCENES
Dan and Noah shooting a
scene for "The Incident."
April 10, 2019

305

BEHIND THE SCENES
Emily posing in her Larry Air uniform.
June 4, 2019

Behind the Episode

Stevie at a crossroads.

EMILY HAMPSHIRE: Stevie went through every kind of personal growth a woman can go through in the last two seasons of the show. I feel a lot of it was her knowing that she could be more than just the girl behind the desk. Ultimately, what the writers wrote for Stevie in season six was so good, because she didn't have to prove anything. She didn't have to go to New York and become a big success there, which I think would have been easy for them to do with Stevie—Stevie goes off to New York and becomes a big "whatever"! Instead, she kind of learned the lesson, which is my favorite of all time, that, like Glinda the Good Witch says, it was always in you. You had the power in you all along, you just had to find it for yourself. And I think that's Stevie's journey.

A WORD TO THE WISE

Johnny Rose's 10 Rules of Business

1

DON'T SPEND YOUR MONEY ALL AT ONCE.

2

SOMETIMES YOU LEAD AND SOMETIMES YOU FOLLOW.

3

KEEPING AN EYE ON THE BOTTOM LINE,
THAT'S HOW A BUSINESS GROWS.

4

TO RUN A BUSINESS, YOU HAVE TO BE HERE TO RUN THE
BUSINESS.

5

IT'S ALL ABOUT PLANNING.

6

THERE'S A SOLUTION TO EVERYTHING.

7

YOU CAN'T JUST BUY THINGS FOR YOURSELF AND WRITE
THEM OFF.

8

YOU WANT TO MAKE SURE YOU'RE MAKING GOOD BAGELS
THE REAL WAY.

9

THE SINK DOESN'T FIX ITSELF.

10

IN TIMES OF CRISIS, THE ONE THING WE NEED TO HANG
ONTO IS FAMILY.

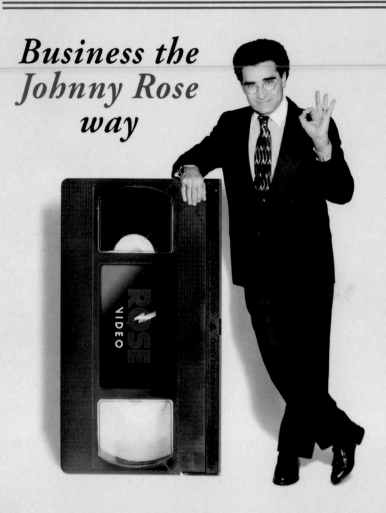

PROP: Johnny Rose's book *Fast Forward to Success*.

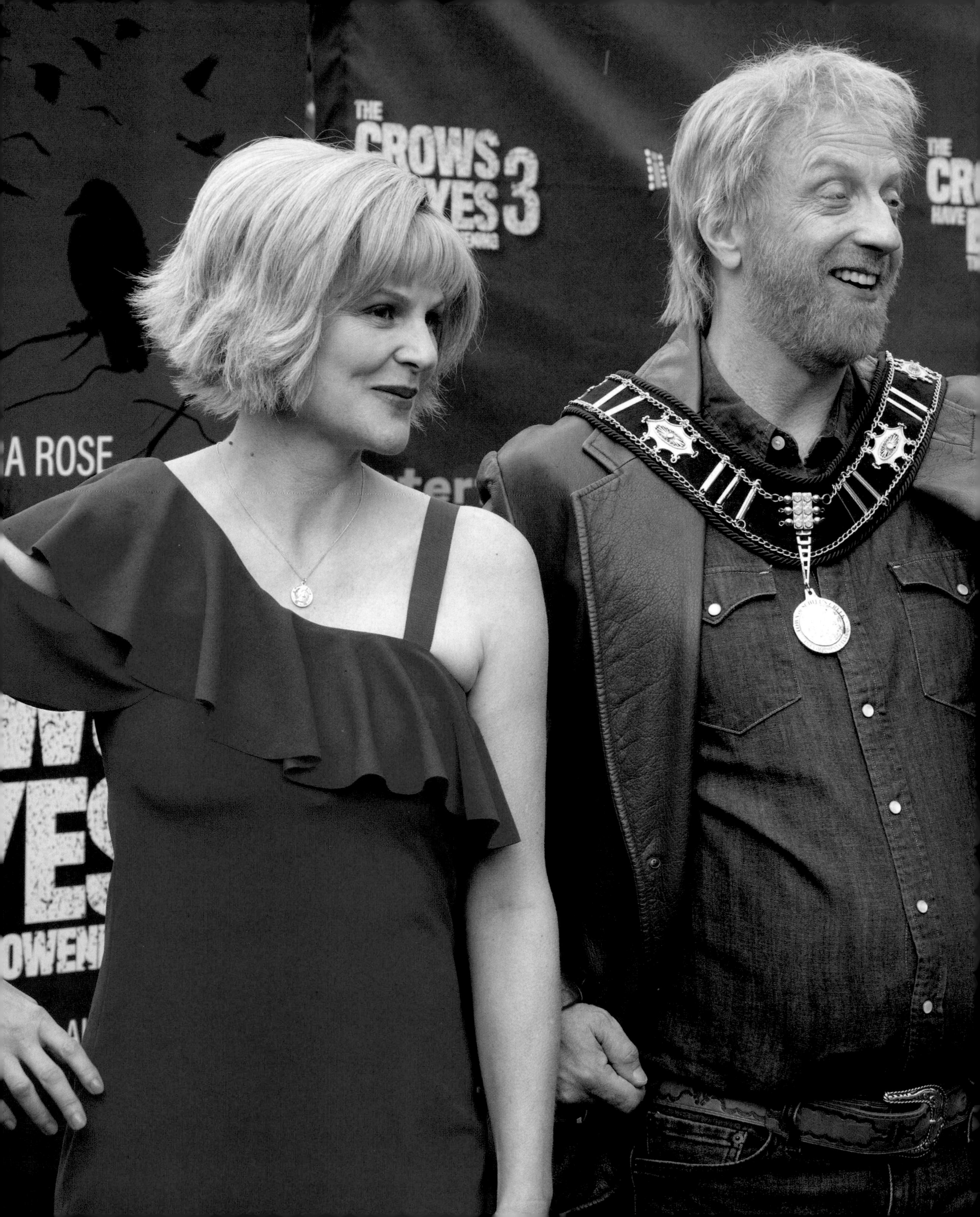
THE
CROWS
3
A ROSE

Behind the Episode

605 THE PREMIERE

Ronnie does the red carpet.

KAREN ROBINSON: I love the little surprises from Ronnie over the years. I love that throughout five and a half seasons you saw Ronnie in her comfortable jeans and her cotton shirts, or a button-up, if she was dressing up. Other than that, she really didn't stray far from what was expected. And then you see her at the *Crows* premiere in a sparkling dress and heels, and you go, *"Oh!"*

The older I get, the more I learn the lesson of "you just never know." You never know where people are coming from, and you don't know what they're capable of. I think Ronnie turning out at the red carpet surprised the hell out of a lot of people.

DEBRA HANSON: We'd only ever seen Ronnie in her comfortable clothes, so the red carpet would be a moment when she would surprise everyone by coming out and being glamorous. I always felt that Ronnie was a very self-assured woman and that she would welcome this opportunity to say, "I'm here. You're not the only stylish people in this town."

What we found, though, was that we had to be selective about picking Ronnie's dress. If you've seen Karen Robinson on red carpets lately, you know that she looks spectacular in clothes. Dan felt that most of the dresses we were putting Karen in were just too glamorous, because Karen could make those pieces look glamorous very, very quickly. So it was a fine balance between finding Ronnie a dress that would dazzle people but not feel unrealistic. We still wanted her to look like Ronnie from Schitt's Creek on the red carpet.

"THE CROWS HAVE EYES AND YOU BETTER NOT LOOK THEM IN IT."

THE CROWS HAVE EYES 3
THE CROWENING
AN INTERFLIX ORIGINAL

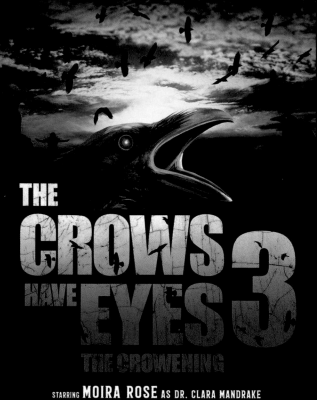

THE CROWS HAVE EYES 3
THE CROWENING

STARRING MOIRA ROSE AS DR. CLARA MANDRAKE

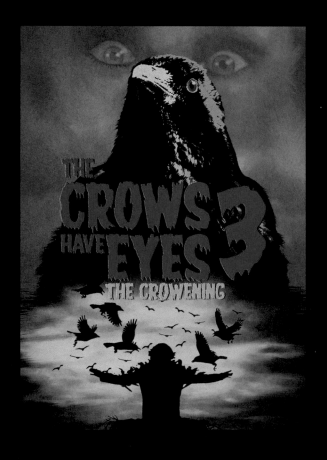

THE CROWS HAVE EYES 3
THE CROWENING

THE CROWS HAVE EYES 3
THE CROWENING

"This is something I directed!" -Blaire   "Delightfully Unhinged!" -Ornithology Today

IN EYE-POPPING TECHNICOLOR!

On a scale of 1 to 10. **THIS FILM IS #1!!!** Rotten Tomatoes

THE CROWS HAVE EYES III
-THE CROWENING-
starring *MOIRA ROSE*
as *Dr. Clara Mandrake*
NOW STREAMING ON INTERFLIX

THE CROWS HAVE EYES III:

the Crowening
STARRING MOIRA ROSE

WORST DIRECTOR   BEST ACTRESS   STARRING MOIRA ROSE

THE CROWS HAVE EYES III

"A TIMELY ALLEGORY ABOUT PREJUDICE"
★★★★★

"IT'S AN APOCALYPTIC FANTASY ABOUT MUTANT CROWS"
★

COMING...IDEALLY SOMETIME THIS YEAR

HOLLYWOOD PRESENTS A BLAIRE PRODUCTION IN ASSOCIATION WITH BOSNIA TOURIST OFFICE CREATED BY THATLIAMSMITH

MOIRA ROSE

"DEAR GOD, WHAT HAVE WE DONE?!"

THE CROWS HAVE EYES 3
THE CROWENING

Starring Moira Rose as Dr. Clara Mandrake • Written and Directed by Blaire
Produced by Crows Eyes III Productions Ltd. Co., Incorporated
Distributed Internationally by Interflix, Inc.

Interflix   R RESTRICTED FOR EXTREME BIRD VIOLENCE
NO CROWS WERE HARMED IN THE MAKING OF THIS FILM. SHOT ENTIRELY IN THE BOSNIAN RIVIERA

(ABOVE , CLOCKWISE FROM TOP LEFT) **FAN ART BY JASON BRUECK, MARY GIBSON, JOE P. FIELDS, LIAM SMITH**
LEFT, CLOCKWISE FROM TOP LEFT) **FAN ART BY VANESSA SEIXAS, NICK CURRY GRAPHICS, JESSICA BUNNELL, SIA TALAVERA**

Behind the Episode

607 **MOIRA ROSÉ**

The talk.

EUGENE LEVY: Johnny having "the talk" with Patrick in episode 607 was a scene I couldn't wait to shoot. I was a major fan of Noah Reid from the day he started work on our show. He is a gifted actor who made it all look so easy. Unfortunately, I was written into very few scenes with him, so when this gem of a scene was handed to me, I jumped at it with relish. From an actor's standpoint, it had all the earmarks of the kind of scene that gets one excited. It was funny. And it was heartfelt.

Johnny has to welcome Patrick into the family, mano a mano. Patrick is engrossed in the baseball game, so Johnny has to fake interest in the game to make the conversation seem more manly and matter-of-fact. Every time Johnny takes a stab at the subject, Patrick sidesteps and dismisses it. But then Patrick eases the pain of Johnny's discomfort by bringing up the subject at hand—his love for David. He assures Johnny that he will protect David and adds just how proud he will be to be a member of the Rose family. It was a funny yet beautiful, emotionally choreographed scene with a great partner.

As a dad, this scene struck a chord. Parents only want the best for their kids. And when it comes to a relationship, they want to know that the people who their kids are in love with are in love with them. Parents want to know that their kids will be protected and not be taken advantage of. They want to know that happiness and security are in their future. And that's exactly what "the talk" said to me. As a dad it gave me comfort, and this scene turned out to be one of the highlights of my six seasons on the show.

BEHIND THE SCENES
Noah in makeup for "The Presidential Suite." April 17, 2019
(RIGHT) Selects from David and Patrick's engagement photo shoot.
Photo credit: Ray Butani.

ALEXIS	This might come as a shock to you, Ted, but I can't move to the Galapagos.
TED	I wouldn't have let you even if you tried. You're building something special here, Alexis, and you deserve to see where it takes you. I'm so proud of you.
ALEXIS	I'm so proud of you. I'd like to think that we helped each other get here.
TED	I know that we did.
ALEXIS	And when you get on that plane tomorrow, I want you to know how grateful I am to have met you.
TED	I don't think I'll ever find another woman who makes me feel the way that you do.
ALEXIS	I'm sure there will be like . . . some other woman . . . somewhere.
TED	Can't say that we didn't try.
ALEXIS	I love you, Ted.
TED	I love you, too. To us.
ALEXIS	To us.

BEHIND THE SCENES
Annie on set for "The Presidential Suite."
April 16, 2019

Behind the Episode

Alexis and Ted say goodbye.

ANNIE MURPHY: As bummed as both Dustin and I were when we found out that Ted and Alexis were not going to end up together, I think it really was the right decision in the end. I was proud to be able to be a part of this scene and this relationship. I think something that isn't talked about enough is that if a relationship ends, it doesn't mean it was a failure. I think this relationship demonstrated that Ted and Alexis loved each other so deeply. They changed *with* each other, not *for* each other. They both taught each other so much. Each of them wanted the other to be happy and each knew that their trajectories were different and they had to let each other go because of that. I don't think those endings are seen enough on TV or in movies, so it was a really special ending for me.

In these last scenes we were not only saying goodbye to the character, but also saying goodbye to the actor. It was Dustin's last day on set. After six years with someone and loving them so much and loving working with them so much, it really was saying goodbye to each other. I remember when we finished shooting, Eugene walked onto set and he had tears streaming down his face and he just opened his arms to me. A weeping Eugene Levy is one of the worst things. And I was like, "Okay, I can no longer be around you or look at you, because I need to get through the rest of this take and you are banished!" But there really was a different kind of energy on set that day.

BEHIND THE SCENES
The cast on set for "Bachelor Party."
May 7, 2019

BEHIND THE SCENES

Baby pictures of Dan (LEFT) and Noah (RIGHT) were used as props for "The Bachelor Party." May 6, 2019
(LEFT) Dan, Sarah, and Eugene on set for "The Bachelor Party." May 7, 2019

Behind the Episode

612 **THE PITCH**

Team Rosebud.

EUGENE LEVY: "The Pitch" was perhaps the most important episode in the series for Johnny. Harnessing his skills and talent as a CEO had been the key in managing his family's survival during their years in Schitt's Creek. Partnering with Stevie and initiating improvements in the motel was a giant step to that end. It eventually took the motel from the red to the black and turned out to be the stepping-stone that led to the idea of expansion. Now, an opportunity has presented itself where that skill and talent would be called upon to sell a concept of a national motel franchise that could be the saving grace for his family. It was an opportunity in which failure was not an option.

After their initial attempt at the pitch gets off to a bumpy start, Johnny manages to rally his shaken troops, muster his business acumen, and stroll back into the boardroom with the confidence to get the pitch back on track. Which he skillfully does. His success at the end of the meeting is a turning point for the Roses and in particular for Johnny. His self-confidence returns. His ability to believe in himself returns. He finally accomplishes what he set out to do from the first day the Roses set foot in Schitt's Creek: to right the terrible wrong that befell his family.

This episode was also a major turning point for Roland. As many times as he feigned boredom at the mention of Rose Video, joked about Johnny taking down his own business, and criticized Johnny's management of the motel, Roland, to our surprise, turns out to be a staunch and supportive friend to Johnny Rose. Defending Johnny to the execs who had been laughing behind Johnny's back was a sign of how closely Roland had bonded with Johnny over the years, and just how much respect he actually had for him. And it showed a dramatic side of Chris Elliott, on camera, that I had never seen before.

EMILY HAMPSHIRE: Mr. Rose treats Stevie like he is the father you dream of, but most people don't have. A lot of people ask me, "Where does Stevie come from and who's her mom and who's her dad?" and I don't know. I usually think about those things for my characters, but for Stevie I never did. I just felt like Stevie was on her own and that was going to be fine. She didn't know what she was missing. She didn't know what it was like to have a Eugene, the ultimate dad. But even though it started out as a father-daughter kind of relationship, sometimes Stevie seemed to be the parent or the one able to see the reality of things. Stevie and Mr. Rose ultimately ended as partners. And that was really special. When we're walking down the aisle together at David's wedding, we're partners, we're equals.

BEHIND THE SCENES
On location for "The Pitch."
June 26, 2019

FAN ART BY FRANCESCA DESCANO

Behind the Episode

A Jazzagals farewell.

JENNIFER ROBERTSON: When you shoot six seasons of a show, a lot of those days become a blur, but shooting the scene where Moira breaks the news to the Jazzagals that she is leaving for New York is still very clear to me. I remember we were all wearing our NYC t-shirts, and I remember Dan coming on set wondering if it was possible if I could be a little less sad. It was difficult, we were all sad. I could see it on the faces of all my sweet Jazzagals. We knew as our characters and as actors that this magical journey was coming to an end. We were no longer going to witness the magic of Catherine O'Hara as Moira sashaying into a Jazzagals rehearsal. The Jazzagals are all different women who found common ground in music. This is what music does, it brings people together. These women loved each other, supported each other, and sang their hearts out. I will always cherish being a Jazzagal.

KAREN ROBINSON: Look, the Jazzagals is a serious community choir. We'll survive Moira's departure. If we didn't, we wouldn't be worthy of Schitt's Creek citizenry. That said, Moira's flair for creating, finding, and fostering the drama in absolutely everything will certainly be missed. And her announcement came as a surprise, caught us off-guard.

The response was exactly what can happen when your heart breaks without warning: shock, dismay, emotion, and an attempt at recovery. What I especially loved was that Moira was going to miss us too. We'd been her safe harbor. Oh, my heart.

SARAH LEVY: The scene when Moira says goodbye to the Jazzagals was a bittersweet one. This was a group of women we'd spent countless hours with learning intricate harmonies for every song we sang. Every aspect of the Jazzagals felt very real, which was why this moment stung a little bit more than I thought it would. Saying goodbye to Moira meant that it was almost time for us to say goodbye to each other as well.

CATHERINE O'HARA: I believe what I said to the Jazzagals in our goodbye scene was sincere for Moira. Never before had she felt so accepted and protected by "friends" as she has by these lovely women. I'm sure she would stay in touch with them after leaving the town, and perhaps even talk someone into making a Jazzagals album. I don't doubt Johnny and Moira would return to see their friends under the guise of just checking in on David and Patrick.

SARAH LEVY: There's a wonderful reveal for Twyla at the end of our last season that I absolutely loved. We learn that, having won the lottery several years ago, Twyla is, in fact, a multi-millionaire. Our audience had come to know and love Twyla for the simplicity of her life and how much joy working at the café, and serving her community brought to her. So when we learn that she had all of this money, but it didn't affect the way she chose to live her life, I think we end up loving her all the more for it.

You could ask a lot of questions about why she didn't do certain things with that money, including offering it to the Roses. I think, either consciously or unconsciously, Twyla had an innate understanding of the fact that sometimes you have to learn lessons in a different way other than just by throwing money at a problem. That was the trouble with the Roses to begin with. Maybe we didn't see it in the beginning when the Roses first came to Schitt's Creek, but Twyla was so wise, and she knew all along that money was never really what the Roses needed. I can't imagine how satisfying and gratifying it was for her to see where they ended up without a pile of cash to rescue them.

I think that's why, in the end, Twyla wanted to offer Alexis the money. She had seen her dear friend come so far all on her own; she was going to a city without her parents and starting a business and doing all of these things that Twyla knew firsthand had taken so much courage for her to earn. I think Twyla finally wanted to support her friend when it didn't feel like she was enabling her for the wrong reasons. And for Alexis to end up turning down the money was just greater confirmation of how deep her transformation had been while living in Schitt's Creek.

Shooting this last scene with Annie was so emotional for our characters and for us. We've seen these two women grow so close over the years. All those conversations at the counter about work and relationships. I think it's perfect that the person Twyla chose to tell her secret to was Alexis. And, of course, I feel the same way about Annie. We grew so close over our six seasons and I just adore her. We broke down in tears and hugged for a long time at the end of this scene.

ANNIE MURPHY: The last scene in the café with Alexis and Twyla, when Twyla confides in Alexis that she has been a multimillionaire all this time, is so triumphant and made me fall in love with Twyla even more. Twyla has helped Alexis in so many ways over the six seasons, none of which involved giving her money to help solve her problems. The fact that she could have shoveled a bunch of money Alexis's way, but chose to give of herself instead is, to me, such a sign of true friendship. I'm also so proud of Alexis for choosing to stand on her own and not take the money that Twyla offers her in their last scene together, even though I think Twyla is offering the money because she believes in Alexis and is proud of her for all the ways she's grown in Schitt's Creek. I love that Twyla says, "I respect that," when Alexis, somewhat reluctantly(!), says no thank you to the money. I think that moment shows so much admiration and respect between these two women who have become such good friends.

I remember when we got to the set that day, Sarah was given the prop envelope, which had an actual prop check inside. Sarah took out the check, looked at it, and was absolutely appalled to discover that it was made out for something like $50,000! She was like, "What?! This is bullshit!" She just couldn't believe that Twyla would be that cheap given how many millions of dollars she had at her disposal. So, Sarah ran off set, found a pen and added a whole bunch of zeroes to the check.

When we went to shoot the scene, there were a whole lot of tears. This scene was my first really big cry. It was a real goodbye between our characters and also between me and Sarah, who I love so much. It was such a tough and wonderful and special scene to shoot with her.

DAVID	No, I was just thinking about how Patrick must have driven out here, and knocked on that door and asked those people to call him if they ever planned on selling, just because I said it was nice. Who does that?
STEVIE	Good people. Good people do things like that. Hence the reason why we don't understand it. Can I ask you a question?
DAVID	Yes.
STEVIE	What is it about New York?
DAVID	I have big dreams.
STEVIE	And you can't have those dreams here?
DAVID	And some friends left there.
STEVIE	The "friends" who you invited to the wedding?
DAVID	To name a few, yes.
STEVIE	David, they're not coming. Apparently, there was an electronic music festival in Norway that took priority. Why do you want to go back to a place that's done nothing but hurt your feelings?
DAVID	Because I want those people to know that I'm not a joke. And that I've won.
STEVIE	David, look at this place. You won!

BEHIND THE SCENES
Dan and Emily on location shooting David and Stevie's
last scene together in "Start Spreading the News."
June 12, 2019

BEHIND THE SCENES
Emily and Dan at the season six wrap party.

Behind the Episode

"David, look at this place. You won!"

DANIEL LEVY: We made the decision to wrap up our characters in the second-to-last episode so we could have fun in the last episode and leave people feeling joyful instead of sad. We knew that there had to be a moment with David and Stevie where we celebrated their friendship and honored how far they've come together. The scene on the hood of Stevie's car was a great bookend to the end of the first season, where David was trying to convince Stevie to go to New York and Stevie had to be so vulnerable with him about why she didn't want to go. It was nice to have David be the vulnerable one this time around.

This moment is the most revealing David has ever been in the series and it just felt like Stevie was the character to be there to see that. I found myself feeling so sad for David that he had been so conflicted by what he assumed other people thought of him. It really did some damage on the poor guy. To have Stevie be the one to remind him that he has made a life for himself here and that's all that really matters now was significant.

On a personal level, it was our last scene together, so as friends it was a tough scene to do. Emily and I have formed such a strange and wonderful familial relationship over these past six years. She means the world to me, so it was an honor to get to have that very raw, very intimate scene with someone I love so much. I think we wanted to make it as good as it could possibly be . . . while also just trying not to slide off the hood of the car!

EMILY HAMPSHIRE: I think this scene was one of the hardest ones for me because the friendship between David and Stevie is so similar to the six years of friendship between Dan and me. In thinking of how far these characters have come, I naturally started to think of how far Dan and I had come. Dan was brilliant in that scene. I remember at the beginning of *Schitt's Creek,* he'd say, "I'm not an actor. You guys are all real professional actors, and I'm just learning from you." To see the truly great actor he had become in that moment just killed me. I couldn't take my eyes off of him, and I was so proud. In that moment, I felt like I was David after Stevie's *Cabaret* number thinking, "THAT'S MY FRIEND!"

We are gathered here today to celebrate the love between two people, whose lives were ostensibly brought together by the fated flap of a butterfly wing. It's practically impossible to explain why things happen the way they do. Our lives are like little bébé crows, carried by an uncertain wind. And all we can wish, for our families and those we love, is that that wind eventually places us on solid ground. And I believe it's done just that for my family here. In this little town. In the middle of nowhere.

Hiccup.
Good. — Are you alright?
— I'm fine. Welcome, everyone, to the wedding.

THE MARRIAGE OF
PATRICK BREWER
AND
DAVID ROSE

Behind the Episode

Wedding Day.

KAREN ROBINSON: The wedding itself was absolutely life- and love-affirming, in a way that was both intensely personal and fabulously universal. Love is love. Between two people, in families, in community, and in the world that embraced our little show and welcomed us into their hearts.

NOAH REID: The wedding day was incredibly special. The Town Hall transformed into an idyllic wedding venue, the Jazzagals singing a choral arrangement of "The Best," Ray and his camera, Moira and her papal hat—it was emotional. Dan cried the whole day. I remember thinking that we were in the midst of making television history and how proud I was to be a part of it.

RIZWAN MANJI: I didn't expect to get emotional when we shot the wedding scene. It wasn't the final day of shooting, so I wasn't pre-programmed to know that I should be upset, but it just sort of happened. It was the culmination of six years of this story, the show, and everything that the show had become. I surprised myself because I am not usually that emotional, but then again, Ray did introduce David and Patrick. So, it makes sense that Ray would also be getting emotional at the wedding. In addition to everything else he did in the town, Ray was also the matchmaker. Add that to his résumé!

EUGENE LEVY: David and Patrick's wedding scene was the culmination of a week of saying goodbye to the sets we had grown to love over the six years of shooting *Schitt's Creek*. Tears were shed when David and Stevie finished their last scene in David's motel room. Alexis and Twyla broke down and hugged after their last encounter in Café Tropical. The Rose family got misty-eyed at the end of their last scene in Johnny and Moira's room. The attachment to those locations we were saying goodbye to was quite tangible. By the time we got to our very last day on the Town Hall set for the wedding scene, the cast and, yes, the crew, were riding an emotional roller coaster from the beginning of the day to the very end.

CATHERINE O'HARA: We were all very emotional on the day of the wedding. Thankfully, Moira was allowed to cry on camera. All I had to do was look around the room at all the wonderful people—cast, crew, and townsfolk—with whom I'd shared six years of hard work and even harder laughs, and, of course, focus on dear David and Patrick sharing their happy love for each other, and both Moira's and my tears flowed nonstop all day long.

Simply The Best

Arranged for the Jazzagals of Schitt's Creek

Arr. AARON JENSEN

BEHIND THE SCENES

Original sheet music for the Jazzagals' arrangement of "The Best" by Aaron Jensen.

Behind the Episode

"You're not crying today."

SARAH LEVY: Shooting the wedding was an incredibly emotional experience, as it was our last day on our sets. It was a very beautiful scene to begin with, and that was matched by the incredibly special and romantic set design of the Town Hall. The versions of "The Best" and "Precious Love" that the Jazzagals sang tipped it over the edge for me. We had to record it live on the day in front of the cast and crew, and everyone was weeping. Try getting through that while watching your dad and brother cry—it was really tough.

AARON JENSEN: I'll never forget sitting backstage and watching the wedding procession on the monitors—hearing the Jazzagals singing the arrangements of "The Best" and "Precious Love." So much had led up to this moment. Not just the arc of the show, but also the friendships and relationships that had blossomed over the years. Everyone was so emotionally invested. You could hear a pin drop during the vows. I treasure my memories from that day.

ANNIE MURPHY: I remember going in and seeing the Town Hall all decorated, and then sitting in the pews (or folding chairs!) while the Jazzagals rehearsed their songs. I was fighting with myself, because I was already in full, basic bridal makeup, and I was like, "You're not crying. You're not crying today. Nope, no sirree." And then I looked back and saw Eugene gazing lovingly at Sarah and tearing up, and I was like, "Oh, well! We're all really screwed now."

ANATOMY OF A LOOK

CATHERINE O'HARA: I grew to expect Debra and Ana could bring to life any idea we might have. For example, miters are not the most comfortable headwear. I also know I look better with a wide rather than a tall hat. So, when it came time to plan Moira's headwear and hair for "Happy Ending," I asked Ana if she could make me a large hair-covered roll to place between me and the miter. We talked about how it might be done, but all I did was talk. Ana, on the other hand, worked for several nights at home to make the hair roll a reality. I had no idea she had put so much work into the piece until she was putting it on my head. She didn't complain at all, but I apologized for taking her talents for granted. Ana also put many hours into the long, blond waves for the look.

ANA SORYS: When Catherine and I started talking about Moira's hair for the wedding, I knew she wanted a miter with some kind of halo effect. I showed her a reference photo of hair that was arranged in a circle and looked a bit like a halo. We decided to go for it and we decided that the hair halo would be Moira's own hair color.

I worked on that halo for what seemed like forever, but it was really only for about a month before we had to shoot the scene. The basic idea for the construction of the halo was to take what amounts to a stuffed tubular stocking, measured to the edge of the tiara where it would sit on Catherine's head. The hair had to fold around the tube, but when you fold hair, it immediately starts to separate and do things you don't want it to do. In order to secure it, I tried sewing it. I tried gluing it. I finally found the one adhesive that didn't make the hair dry and crispy, and still left a sheen and softness to it. It was the spray glue that I used on my kitchen tiles! I had to spray it down and let it dry after each layer. It was a process, but it worked in the end.

No one really knew what Catherine was going to look like in that piece, not even Dan. So when she walked out on set and everyone saw her look, they gasped. That was the highlight of my career. Just watching people enjoy that look.

DEBRA HANSON: We talked a lot about the costuming for Moira in the wedding scene. The original assumption was that her ensemble was going to be black. I thought, "It has to be ecclesiastical and it has to be a showstopper." I spent a lot of time looking for black dresses, but I just wasn't finding anything I liked because I also really wanted a feeling of spirituality and of lightness. So, I was scrolling and scrolling through sites and then I remember I clicked on a particular dress and said, "Oh my god." It was McQueen. It was cream colored. It looked like a bishop's robe. And, what you see for only one brief shot in the episode is that when you turn to the back of the dress, it has wings. I knew this was the dress.

I have a wonderful milliner who I asked to create the miter to go with it. As for the jewelry, what we were finding is that most of the pieces we were working with were too heavy, or they pointed too much toward history or religion, and not fashion. Fortunately, my kit is full of jewelry from other shows. We pulled one piece, put it on backward, and it worked! If we put it on the right way it was terrible, but the back of the piece was beautiful and had an indescribable twinkle to it. When we put everything together on Catherine, with Ana's Lady Godiva wig, we all knew it was the perfect look.

LUCKY BROMHEAD: As I was reading the script for "Happy Ending," I knew that there was going to be a lot of emotion for Moira. Catherine is such a brilliant performer that it's never about needing the usual makeup artist tricks for tears, like adding a bit of menthol under the eye or dropping in a fake tear. Catherine cries, every time. She taps into those emotions, so every single take we did that day, she was crying for real.

For this scene we wanted Moira to look like LOVE personified. We changed the shape of her eye a bit and gave her skin more glow. We kept the iconic shape of her mouth, but swapped her trademark red lipstick for something a little more angelic. When it came to her eyes, though, we knew there was an opportunity to contrast her iconic black eye makeup with her ethereal look. We loved the idea that as Moira became emotional you would see these black tears marring her perfect face. We weren't intentionally thinking that this would be an iconic look, but images of Moira in her wedding ensemble with black lines running down her face have become iconic.

BEHIND THE SCENES
Catherine O'Hara captured here, preparing for the wedding scene.

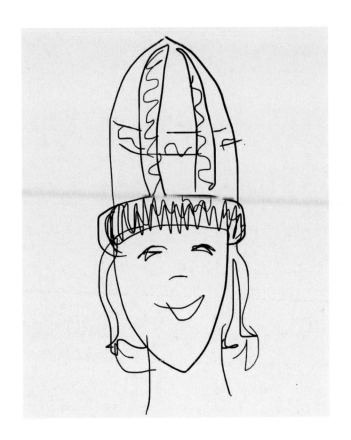

BEHIND THE SCENES
Catherine O'Hara's original sketch for Moira's miter and wig.
(LEFT) Ana Sorys and Catherine perfecting Moira's wedding look.
May 15, 2019

Behind the Episode

614 HAPPY ENDING

Saying goodbye to our sets.

DANIEL LEVY: Our last day on set was the wedding. There was a kind of nostalgic dust in the air that was beautiful and sad at the same time. It felt like we were honoring the show that day. We were all together, the entire cast, and all dressed up because of the wedding. Normally, you would only have two or four actors working at a time, so to have everybody there really made it feel festive and special. I think the bittersweet nature of the day, knowing that we were saying goodbye to our sets, only helped the emotional tension of the wedding scene.

And then, it wrapped. The day was done. We had champagne. We offered our gratitude to the sets. I spent the rest of the night wandering around the sets that I'd come to know as my second home. It was surreal to think back to the early days before we had a show, when we were in pre-production and Brendan and I were dreaming up how each set would look and feel. Everything from the paintings on the walls to the color of the carpet, the way the beds looked, the turquoise tiles, the color of the wood and the wallpaper in the bathrooms. I was walking through and saying goodbye to an experience that had completely transformed me creatively. I was also eying the sets to see if there was anything sentimental I could steal.

I eventually wandered into David and Alexis's motel room and discovered Annie in there. We just looked at each other and completely fell apart. I had cried on and off throughout the entire last season, because I'm a crier and generally a mess, but Annie had been incredibly stoic. In that moment, though, we both knew that the end was near and our hearts couldn't take it. We just hugged each other and cried. My sister, Sarah, walked in right at that moment and took this picture. Looking at it now, it's as if I'm right back there. The photo now hangs on my office wall. A bittersweet memory I will never forget.

BEHIND THE SCENES
Annie and Dan at the end of the final day on set.
May 15, 2019

Behind the Episode

The last day of shooting.

EMILY HAMPSHIRE: The final scene was our last day on location. Everyone was crying before we even got to set, but I was channeling Stevie saying, "Yeah, it doesn't affect me when I end a show." Two seconds later, Mr. Rose comes over to hug me, and I'm bawling my eyes out.

The story may be fiction, but after six seasons the relationships are *real!* Mr. Rose's relationship with Stevie is as true to me as my real-life relationship with Eugene. It's a double heartbreak to say goodbye to these characters and the relationships they have on the show and to also know we're saying goodbye to each other. It was bittersweet because I think we all realized how lucky we are to have been part of this show and have each other in our real lives. We genuinely like each other. It was this art–life dynamic that I think is the loveliest, most special thing I've ever experienced.

NOAH REID: If I thought the wedding day was emotional, shooting this scene on location in front of the motel was a whole other gear. People couldn't even look at each other without breaking into tears. Eugene was heroic that day, keeping it together and keeping it moving while everyone was just falling apart. I tried to follow his lead, but I'm not sure how successful I was. Somehow we got through it together, and we ended the night drinking champagne in the parking lot and hugging each other through tears.

ANNIE MURPHY: Saying goodbye to Johnny and Moira was also us saying goodbye to Eugene and Catherine and the show. I had been shoving down the emotions as much as possible that day just to get through it, but then we got to the last rehearsal of the last scene on the last day. The levee finally broke, if you will, and I remember looking over and seeing the look of absolute glee on Dan's face. He had been breaking down all day and was getting really upset that I was keeping it together. Finally, I got my comeuppance.

I'm so glad the last scene was scheduled the way it was, because there was a lot of real reaction and real emotion. I'm so glad those moments are in a time capsule now.

DANIEL LEVY: Shooting on the last day was tricky because I knew that if I started to get upset, it wouldn't stop, and we had an entire day to shoot. I was also codirecting that episode, there was just a lot that needed to get done. And, yet, I knew: "By the end of this day, we will have finished this show." So, I was doing great, doing great, doing great, until we started to block and rehearse the scene where Johnny and Moira say goodbye to the family. I looked over at Annie in the rehearsal and she was just gone. Like *gone* gone, like I'd never seen. And that of course made me cry, but it also made me sadistically happy because I'd been waiting for the day that would happen to her. It was a good thing, because by the time we got to shoot the scene, it was still very emotional, but we had gotten the extreme catharsis out of the way.

Behind the Episode

"Applause. Tears. Hugs."

EUGENE LEVY: I knew it was going to be tough to get through our Rose family goodbye scene. Our characters saying goodbye to each other would really be us saying goodbye to each other, and to a show that we all adored and could not have been more proud of. Saying goodbye to David, Patrick, Alexis, and Stevie was an emotionally draining experience. Take after take, it never got easier. Shooting the last scene on the road looking back from our limousine for the very last time at the town sign, which now featured the Rose family faces looking back at me, was another tough moment.

The entire cast was shooting that day, as we had three scenes scheduled, which meant that every single person working in front of and behind the camera would be there for a final goodbye. Each time an actor completed their final scene, our first AD, Mark Pancer, would make an announcement with a quiver in his voice: "Ladies and gentlemen, she's the best sister ever, that's a wrap, a series wrap for Annie Murphy." The applause from cast and crew was loud and long. Annie sobbed, and tears streamed down our cheeks. "Ladies and gentlemen, that's a series wrap on Dan Levy." Applause. Tears. Hugs. And so it went, into the night. And after we wrapped, we uncorked the champagne and toasted each other. We all knew, no matter what the future held for us, there would never be another *Schitt's Creek*.

Behind the Episode

614 **HAPPY ENDING**

On saying goodbye.

KAREN ROBINSON: The last day of shooting was at the Rosebud Motel. It was a washout for me weeping-wise and a beautiful finale to a wonder-filled period of my life that I'm still struggling to process.

SARAH LEVY: The very last day of shooting is almost a blur despite any attempt to remain present and take it all in. It felt like the last day of high school; it was such a celebration and a heartbreak all at once with lots and lots and lots of hugs and tears. A very bittersweet, special day.

RIZWAN MANJI: I had my cathartic emotional moment at the wedding, so I was able to have a really fun time on the last day of shooting. I remember sitting with Eugene at a table outside the apothecary and thinking, "Look at how far we've come in six years. Look at all of these people that I've so enjoyed working with." It was a very good and surreal experience.

JENNIFER ROBERTSON: During the last two days of shooting I tried to take moments and tuck them away in my heart. Sitting with Eugene at the Boston Pizza having a glass of wine while we waited for everyone else to show up or having a sleepover with Annie on the last night in the hotel and seeing the pile of bobby pins on her bedside table that she took out the night before from her Alexis hairstyle.

On the last day I was in a daze, looking around at the cast and crew and asking myself, "How will I get through next year not spending part of it with all these fine people?"

ANDREW CIVIDINO, DIRECTOR: I remember our last day vividly. We all wanted to hold on to every single scene and every single take as the day moved on, because we just weren't ready for the show to be over yet.

The goodbyes we captured on screen are real. If anything, I felt that my biggest job behind the camera was to make sure I didn't let my own emotions get in the way of what was best for the show. I remember we actually had to dial back on some of the farewells at one point because the layered emotion of parting ways both as the Roses, and as a cast and crew that grew to be a family over six seasons, was so deeply felt.

BEHIND THE SCENES
One last look at the Rosebud Motel after the after party.
June 27, 2019

Dan behind the scenes at the wedding.

Eugene, Annie, Rizwan, Karen, Dan,
and Emily behind the scenes on the last day.

Chris, John, and Eugene enjoying a laugh
while filming "Moira vs. Town Council."

Lucky touching up Catherine's tears
in between takes while filming "Happy Ending."

Dan enjoys a set visit from his dog, Redmond Levy,
the unofficial mascot of Schitt's Creek.

Annie and Emily caught in
an early-morning embrace.

Annie and Catherine sharing a hug after
Catherine officially wrapped the series.

Chris, Jenn, John, Dan, Karen, Rizwan, Catherine, Sarah,
and Eugene behind the scenes of season six.

Behind the scenes of Catherine and Sarah
filming Moira's tourism ad.

Noah, director Andrew Cividino (with back to camera),
and Dan share a laugh during "Life Is a Cabaret,"
while Annie lurks in the background.

Team Schitt's at Toronto Pride, 2018.

Eugene wearing one of Moira's wigs
on the last day of shooting.

Sarah and Karen. Not having fun. At all.

Jenn is all of us after seeing herself in that wig.

Sarah, Annie, Kevin McGarry, Karen, Jenn, and Emily leaning into the power of Elevation while shooting "Moira Rosé."

A piece of set decoration that didn't get quite enough air time during "Merry Christmas, Johnny Rose."

Dan landing on a safety mat while attempting his hundredth dive into home plate during the filming of "The M.V.P."

Dustin blow-drying his armpits in between takes. To his credit, it was a very hot day on set and a grey t-shirt is always a risky move.

Early days of constructing Café Tropical.

The whole gang ready for the 2019 Emmy Awards.

Annie, Sarah, and Jenn behind the
scenes of "Life Is a Cabaret."

John, Karen, Chris, and Eugene take a
break from filming "The Wingman."

Eugene, Catherine, Annie, Karen, Dan,
and Noah moments before making Emmy history.

Emily doing her real job—checking her phone—while
on a break from filming "Life Is a Cabaret."

BEHIND THE SCENES
Eugene and Dan embrace after winning the 2020 Emmy for Outstanding Comedy Series.

THANK YOU

PUTTING THIS BOOK TOGETHER WAS the greatest walk down memory lane and the ultimate reminder of just how much love and care went into getting our show made. Looking back on this life-changing journey was a real testament to the power of hard work, dedication, and community building. To go from not knowing if we would get a second season to becoming the most Emmy-awarded comedy series in a single night is something that we never saw coming. It's proof that sticking to your guns, trusting your instincts, and charting your own path has the potential to change not only your life but the lives of people you may never meet. *Schitt's Creek* can now be seen in 181 countries around the world. So thank you. Thank you to our brilliant crew, who we miss so much. Thank you to our cast, who continue to make us laugh and cry and smile with every rewatch. Thank you to our broadcast networks, who never got in the way and supported us on this uphill climb. Thank you to the publicity team, who carefully and thoughtfully guided us through the past few years. Thank you to everyone who supported this show financially and strategically—affording us the means and the freedom to tell our stories. And again, thank you to all of you—every fan who watched this show and helped get the word out, many of you from the very beginning.

Love that journey for all of us.

–DAN AND EUGENE

THANK YOU to the fan artists, whose work can be seen throughout these pages, as well as to Mychal Tepker of @SchittsSheets and Liz Dyer of Mama Bears. To the fans who contributed photographs of their EW DAVID license plates, and to everyone who contributed their memories, stories, and photographs of the making of the show: Lucky Bromhead, Jordan Canning, Jerry Ciccoritti, Andrew Cividino, Robin Duke, Chris Elliott, Emily Hampshire, Debra Hanson, John Hemphill, Aaron Jensen, Sarah Levy, Rizwan Manji, Dustin Milligan, Cleo Kass Moloney, Annie Murphy, Catherine O'Hara, Noah Reid, Jennifer Robertson, Karen Robinson, Tim Rozon, Amy Segal, Brendan Smith, Ana Sorys. Thank you to the Schitt's Creek team: Ashley Ayre, Calum Shanlin, Deb Divine, Megan Zehmer, Hilary Goldstein; ITV Studios: Emma Sutherley, Shirley Patton, Christina Lima, Temi Oguntade, Thomas Westwood; Black Dog & Leventhal editorial: Becky Koh; Design: Martin Venezky, Susan Van Horn.

CREDITS:

Endpaper art by Ellen Surrey © Pop Media Networks, LLC

@SchittsSheets: p. 60-61, 120, 156-157, 190, 196, 220

Letter from Mama Bears, courtesy of Liz Dyer: p.273

Mama Bears is an organization dedicated to supporting, educating, and empowering families with LGBTQ members and the LGBTQ community. The organization offers a variety of private groups, websites, special projects, and resources. For more info about the organization and how to join the private groups visit the website realmamabears.org.

Arrangement of "The Best" for the Jazzagals, courtesy of Aaron Jensen, ©Countermeasure Music: p. 344

Image of Tweet, courtesy of Mariah Carey: p. 226

PHOTOGRAPHY CREDITS:

Jordan Canning: p. 360 (top right), 363 (bottom left), 364 (top left)

Jerry Ciccoritti: p. 109

Caitlyn Cronenberg: p. 67 (episodes 111, 112)

Emily Hampshire: p. 336

Simon Lee: p. 52-53, 309

Daniel Levy: p. 40-41, 59, 176, 193, 195, 229, 234 (top right), 244 (bottom), 248, 270-271, 325, 358, 360 (top left), 363 (top right)

Sarah Levy: p. 351

Rizwan Manji: p. 161

Cleo Kass Moloney: p. 153

Annie Murphy: p. 262

Catherine O'Hara: p. 345

Brooke Palmer: p. 10, 238-239 (episode 508), 260-261, 286-287 (episodes 603, 607, 708), 317, 361 (bottom right)

Jasper Savage: 185 (episode 409), 219

Amy Segal: 274, 281, 288, 361 (top left), 362 (top right), 364 (bottom left)

Ana Sorys: p. 4, 194, 243, 258, 282, 298, 299, 300, 306, 316, 320, 324, 339, 343, 344, 347, 360 (bottom right), 361 (top right), 362 (bottom left and right), 364 (bottom right), 365 (bottom left and right), 366

Ian Watson: p. 28, 238-239 (*episodes 501, 502, 503, 504, 507, 511*), 240, 241, 272

Steve Wilke: p. 12, 15, 16, 20, 22, 25, 26, 30, 32, 36, 42, 43, 46-47, 48-49, 50-51, 56, 58, 66-67 (*episodes: 101, 102, 103, 104, 105, 106, 107, 108, 109, 110, 113*), 78-79, 82 (top), 92-93, 98-99, 102-103, 104-105, 107, 108, 115, 118, 119, 120, 121 (top right, middle left and right, bottom left), 123, 124, 126-127, 134-135, 138-139 (*episodes 302, 303, 304, 305, 307, 308, 309, 310, 311, 312, 312*), 146, 160, 162-163, 170-171, 173, 174, 178-179, 180-181, 184-185 (*episodes 401, 402, 403, 404, 405, 406, 407, 408, 410, 411, 412, 412*), 186-187, 188-189, 197, 198-199, 201(top), 213, 214-215, 216-217, 219 (top and bottom) 228, 230-231, 234 (top left, bottom right), 238-239 (*episodes 505, 506, 509, 512, 513, 514*), 244 (top), 276-277, 278-279, 283, 286-287 (*episodes 601, 602, 604, 605, 609, 610, 611, 612, 613, 614*), 302, 303, 304-305, 310-311, 322-323, 328, 329, 334-335, 338, 340-341, 348, 352, 355, 362 (top left), 363 (bottom right), 364 (top right, bottom left), 365 (top left and right)

Ken Woroner: p. 19, 138 (episodes 301, 306), 142 (top left and right, middle left, bottom right)

FAN ART CREDITS:

Chris Ables: p. 76, 292

© 2021 Hunter Barrett: p. 205-211, 295-297

Jo Ben-Shmuel, @jobenshmuel.art: p. 116

Jason Brueck: p. 313

Jessica Bunnell/PowerPop Studios: p. 312 (bottom right)

C. Cimoroni: p. 164, 232

Ross Cooke: p. 8

© 2021 Jessica Cruickshank: p. 2, 60-61, 65, 101, 137, 183, 237, 285

© 2021 by Nick Curry Graphics, www.etsy.com/shop/PopCultVulture: p. 312 (top right)

Joe P. Fields, cultpopdesigns.com: p. 313 (bottom right)

Francesca Descano, *FrantasticalCo*: p. 330

Sarah Ferguson, "Moira & Her Girls": p. 191

Rita Garza of RitaWorks Art & Illustration: p. 55, 172

© 2021 Jillian Goeler: p. 6-7, 156-157

Nicholas Holman: p. 44-45

Brandon Lord, @brandonldesign: p. 154

Carla Maskall, @2sistersfanart: p. 140

Cara Mathis: p. 1

LC McDonald of Little Shop of ElleSee: p. 221

Kory McGeehan: p. 120

Carolyn "Charlie" Breen, *Goodwood ON Café "Café Tropical"*: p. 54

Bunny Perno-Horne: p. 125

Greg Robertson: p. 112

Vanessa Seixas: p. 312(top left)

Steve Sizer, @mrstevers p. 155

Original watercolor illustration by Noelle Smith: p. 166

Danielle Sylvan, Sylvan Design Co.: p. 39

Sia Talavera: p. 312 (bottom left)

Justin Teodoro, Artist/Illustrator: p. 110

Susan Van Horn: p. 196, 263

Jess Watson, *Moira Rose "The Dress" 2020 Digital (Procreate)*: p. 246

Kendall Wisniewski: p. 267

COPYRIGHT © 2021

Not A Real Holding Company Inc. Licensed by ITV Studios Limited. All rights reserved.

COVER DESIGN BY SUSAN VAN HORN

COVER COPYRIGHT © 2021 BY HACHETTE BOOK GROUP, INC.

Hachette Book Group supports the right to free expression and the value of copyright. The purpose of copyright is to encourage writers and artists to produce the creative works that enrich our culture.

The scanning, uploading, and distribution of this book without permission is a theft of the author's intellectual property. If you would like permission to use material from the book (other than for review purposes), please contact permissions@hbgusa.com. Thank you for your support of the authors' rights.

BLACK DOG & LEVENTHAL PUBLISHERS

Hachette Book Group
1290 Avenue of the Americas
New York, NY 10104
www.hachettebookgroup.com
www.blackdogandleventhal.com

First Edition: October 2021

Black Dog & Leventhal Publishers is an imprint of Perseus Books, LLC, a subsidiary of Hachette Book Group, Inc. The Black Dog & Leventhal Publishers name and logo are trademarks of Hachette Book Group, Inc.

The publisher is not responsible for websites (or their content) that are not owned by the publisher.

The Hachette Speakers Bureau provides a wide range of authors for speaking events. To find out more, go to www.HachetteSpeakersBureau.com or call (866) 376-6591.

Print book interior design by Martin Venezky/ Appetite Engineers

LCCN 2021934585

ISBNs: 978-0-7624-9950-2 (hardcover); 978-0-7624-7943-6 (ebook); 978-0-7624-7944-3 (ebook); 978-0-7624-9949-6 (ebook); 978-0-7624-8071-5 (signed edition); 978-0-7624-8072-2 (barnesandnoble.com signed edition)

Printed in Canada

TC

10 9 8 7 6 5 4 3